AF863518

THE JESUS KIDS AND THEIR LEADERS

A penetrating, insightful, entertaining survey of the fast-growing religious revival in America today. Written by a veteran writer on contemporary religious trends, this is an honest, deeply-felt review of a controversial, changing scene that will inform and involve every reader. For anyone interested in what our young people are thinking about God and Man, this book is essential, vital reading.

Other Warner Paperback Library Books
By Glenn D. Kittler

Edgar Cayce On The Dead Sea Scrolls
The Peace Corps
Laetrile: Control For Cancer

THE JESUS KIDS AND THEIR LEADERS

By Glenn D. Kittler

WARNER PAPERBACK LIBRARY
NEW YORK

WARNER PAPERBACK LIBRARY EDITION

First Printing: September, 1972

Warner Paperback Library is a division of Warner Books, Inc., 315 Park Avenue South, New York, N.Y. 10010.

To Ruth Williams

CONTENTS

THE JESUS KIDS AND THEIR LEADERS

1

"Jesus Loves You!"

When I telephoned the office of the *Hollywood Free Paper* for the first time, the young man who answered the call greeted me with: "Jesus loves you!" In itself, this was not news to me. I had been raised in a Christian home; I had been given a Christian education. Several of my close friends in boyhood had entered the Catholic clergy, as for a while I thought I would. Also, for twenty years I had been a Roving Editor for *Guideposts Magazine,* the most widely read American publication in the field of religion. And for more years than that, most of the writing I had done—thus most of the thinking I had done—had been in this same area. So I already knew that Jesus loved me, just as I knew that he also loved everyone else.

Even so, this greeting, coming at me as it did, the first thing on an autumn Monday morning in 1971, startled me a bit. It was like unexpectedly stepping into a cold shower. It woke me up. This was, in a way, my first direct contact with what had become known as the Jesus People, and I wasn't prepared for such suddenness. After a moment, I said: "Thank you." Then I asked to speak to Duane Pederson.

For me, this was the beginning of a ten-thousand-mile search for the soul of the Jesus People movement. I felt like a man standing at both ends of a bridge at the same time. In a sense, I already knew what I would find.

My interest in the movement began in 1961 when I learned that John Sherrill, a Senior Editor at *Guideposts* and a close friend for almost ten years, had received the Baptism in the Holy Spirit. I did not know what that meant. John himself said nothing to me about it at the time. But his secretary, knowing how close we were, told me that she was growing considerably disturbed by the unusual memos about the experience which John was dictating on disks for his files. She let me read one. It ran several pages, and it was the basis for the book John eventually wrote, *They Speak With Other Tongues,* published in November, 1964. The memo seemed so personal and was so moving that I realized something important had happened to John; but because of the nature of the experience, I felt this was a subject John would have to broach first. Meanwhile, I decided to find out what I could about it.

What I learned later turned out to be at the very heart of the Jesus People movement. And the heart of the matter was a personal Pentecost.

John Sherrill received the Baptism in the Holy Spirit on December 2, 1960, and with it he received the Gift of

Tongues, sometimes called "speaking in tongues." Formally, this is the glossolalia, and I knew what that was. It was ecstatic prayer in a language which few, if any, understood, and it was a prevalent spiritual practice among the early Christians. In St. Paul's first letter to the Corinthians, probably written early in 57 A.D., he instructed Christians there not to use tongues in public because non-Christians who heard them might think they were all crazy. Paul said he had the gift himself and probably used it as much as anybody, but he felt it should be reserved for private devotions. According to my Catholic training, the glossolalia went out around the third or fourth century; and when it appeared these days it was most likely religious hysteria being experienced by some backwoods Fundamentalists. I wondered what on earth had happened to John.

John took the title for his book from Acts 2:4, which, in King James, reads: "And they were all filled with the Holy Ghost, and began to speak with other tongues, as the Spirit gave them utterances." I had read that passage many times but had always interpreted it in terms of the Douay Catholic Bible, which puts it: "And they were all filled with the Holy Spirit and began to speak in foreign tongues, even as the Holy Spirit prompted them to speak." A Douay footnote explains foreign tongues as "languages unknown to the speakers. Literally, 'different tongues,' i.e., different from their own speech." Acts 2 goes on to say that present at the Pentecost were people from many different Middle East countries, and each understood the Apostles in his own dialect. I had no difficulty accepting that. Throughout Catholic history, numerous saints had the faculty for speaking and understanding foreign languages upon first encountering them, and this was my view of what happened at Pentecost. John's view, expressed in his long memo, was that the Apostles had spoken in the glossolalia and the foreigners were able to interpret them each in his own dialect. As time passed and John said nothing to me about his Baptism, I wondered if, because of our differing views, he preferred not to share with me an experience on which he felt we would basically disagree.

In his book, John said that he originally intended to

write an objective, journalistic appraisal of the Baptism in the Holy Spirit as it was being increasingly experienced in this country, particularly in the Pentecostal-oriented groups. But after he received the Baptism himself, he felt he could no longer be objective, and so he put the book aside until he could decide how he was going to tell the story. About two weeks after this Baptism, John met the Reverend David Wilkerson through a mutual friend. In 1958, Wilkerson, a minister in the Assembly of God, felt summoned by the Holy Spirit to leave his home in a small Pennsylvania town to go to New York City with the teen-age addicts whose gangs were turning the city into a battle-field. His mission: to win their souls for Jesus Christ. Wilkerson had gone to John's office that day because he needed ten thousand dollars to buy a house in Brooklyn for his teen-agers. John didn't have that kind of money, but he knew somebody who did: W. Clement Stone, the Chicago insurance millionaire and philanthropist. I had met Stone when I interviewed him in Chicago for a *Guideposts* article. A publisher then asked me to assist Stone in writing a book about his religious and philosophical convictions. Other work prevented me from doing so; but John and his wife, Elizabeth, took the assignment, and out of the collaboration developed a lasting friendship. The day John met Wilkerson, Stone happened to be in New York. John wrote a note of introduction which Wilkerson took to Stone, and Stone gave Wilkerson the money.

Sometime in 1961, the Sherrills told me they were working on a book with Dave Wilkerson, and they were calling it *The Cross and The Switchblade*. Some of the research interviews were being done in John's office. I thus began to see Wilkerson around when I'd go to the office for editorial meetings; during coffee breaks, we'd talk. Later, when I read the book, I found it hard to believe that this pleasant, shy, gentle, little man could be such a spiritual dynamo.

One afternoon, while the research was still going on, I arrived at the office for a meeting a bit early. The place was unusually quiet. I helped myself to a cup of coffee and I sat at the long table in the central room to study my notes for the meeting. John Sherrill's office was about ten feet away, and the door was shut. Gradually I became aware of a sound, the sound of a man's voice, and it was coming from John's room. Without eavesdropping, I realized that I could not understand what the man was saying. My first impression was that it sounded like a Catholic priest softly chanting a Latin Mass, but I knew that this was unlikely. The voice rose and fell in level and volume. It sounded like Hebrew. It sounded like Portuguese. It sounded like Arabic. And it went on and on.

Puzzled, I got up, went to the office manager's door and asked: "Lois, what's going on in John's office?"

She listened. Then she said: "Dave Wilkerson is in there. Sounds like he's speaking in tongues again."

"Speaking in tongues?"

"Yes." She looked at me as though I should have known.

So that was it. That's what it sounded like. And Dave Wilkerson had it, too.

The Cross and the Switchblade was published in December, 1962. Reading it, I saw clearly that Dave Wilkerson was a strongly Spirit-guided man, but I kept waiting for the part about tongues. Here and there were hints of it, but nothing specific, and I began to wonder if speaking in tongues was supposed to be kept secret. Then, at the end, it all came out. In an almost textbook fashion, Dave Wilkerson gives a lecture on the Baptism and tongues to a Jesuit who evidently knew less about it than I did. But apparently everybody associated with Dave Wilkerson had the gift. Here was this epidemic, practically under my nose, and I hadn't heard of it.

John Sherrill still said nothing to me about himself. Two years later, however, he told me about himself in the way that a writer would: he gave me a copy of his book on tongues.

With that, the subject was out in the open at *Guideposts*. The subject was out in the open, in fact, all over the country. Both Wilkerson's and John's books became bestsellers. Dave Wilkerson was busy opening his Teen Challenge centers for young addicts all over the country, and John became a celebrity in his own right. He was frequently invited to speak to groups interested in the Baptism or already in the Baptism. From time to time, John would tell me that there were some Catholics present at a certain meeting, and I would tell him that there were kooks in every religion. And from time to time, John would say that he had spoken to a group that was entirely Catholic, and I would tell him that I already knew the Church was falling apart.

Some churches were, actually. As the Holy Spirit—Pentecostal, perhaps—movement spread across the country, many churches were divided on the question of whether Pentecostal groups should be allowed to function in the church, even apart from the regular congregational services. Many ministers who allowed young people to hold Pentecostal prayer services anywhere on the church property lost their pulpits. Church leaders, especially Presbyterian and Methodist, could not agree on a view toward the movement. The Catholic hierarchy remained silent. Disgruntled youngsters, unable to worship as they wished in their churches, went elsewhere, and the country began to hear about the Jesus People.

In its cover story—"The Jesus Revolution"—in the issue of June 21, 1971, *Time* said that the one person probably most responsible for the great surge of the Jesus People movement was David Wilkerson, through his book. This is true. But when I read that, I found myself thinking that another person was certainly almost as responsible: John Sherrill, through Wilkerson's book and through his own. I mentioned that to John one day, and he said: "You're wrong. The Holy Spirit is responsible."

It so happened that during the summer of 1960, when John Sherrill was first beginning his research into the Pentecostal movement, I was doing research on a book about the Maryknoll Fathers, the American Catholic missionary society. The Sherrills were living at Chappaqua, about fifty miles north of New York City. The Maryknoll archives were at the motherhouse near Ossining, about ten minutes from the Sherrills. The summer was stifling. The room where I worked was not air conditioned, and the window seemed incapable of getting into the path of a breeze. On days when I finished early or when I just didn't feel like working, I'd call the Sherrills and invite myself over for a cool drink before making the long drive back to the scorching city.

When I first met the Sherrills in 1952, they were Quakers. By 1960, they had become Episcopalians. I often teased them about this, telling them they had only one more step to take to make their way to Rome. That summer, I suggested several times that they take the kids and visit Maryknoll because the place was beautiful and had a fascinating museum. One day they told me that they had made the visit and enjoyed it very much.

Years later, after John's books were published and some of us at *Guideposts* could talk about the Baptism in the Holy Spirit and about speaking in tongues without cringing at the thoughts, I still did not feel involved, believing that these things were a Protestant phenomenon that would soon fade away. I knew there were some Catholics involved; but I also knew some Catholics had been involved in the Reformation, and I knew what this had spawned. No, this was not for me.

Then one evening after an editorial meeting, I had dinner with the Sherrills in town, and at one point John turned to me and asked: "Remember how you used to tease Tibby and me about becoming Catholics?"

"Yes, I do," I said, preparing myself for the good news.

"Well," said John, "I think things are going the other way."

I glanced at both of them. "What do you mean?"

John asked: "Do you still have much contact with the Maryknollers?"

"Not really," I said. "I haven't been up there for years."

John said: "I'll bet we're having more contact with the Maryknollers than you ever did."

This was a hopeful sign. I asked: "Do you go over there much?"

"Yes," said John, "but the Maryknollers are spending more time at our place than we're spending at theirs. And they're all jabbering away in tongues."

I didn't know what to think.

I had always been a believer in coincidence. It was a coincidence that, in 1952, I wrote an article which editors of other magazines thought was too religious for them, and one of them suggested that I send it to *Guideposts*. I had never heard of *Guideposts*. It was a coincidence that the article landed on John's desk. He wrote me, advising me that if I changed the viewpoint of the article from the third person to the first person it might be accepted, although without payment. The article was about a good friend of mine who needed the publicity, and it was because of this coincidence that I made the change, without payment, and the article was accepted. Out of this, John invited me to lunch with him and Len LeSourd, the Executive Editor. Out of this came an invitation to join the staff as a Roving Editor. It was coincidence that I should be drawn more to the Sherrills than to others on the staff; we three shared a keen concern about the craft of writing, and we talked writing more than we talked anything else.

It was a coincidence that I was given the assignment to go to Chicago to interview Clement Stone. My family lived in Chicago, and Len knew that the assignment would give me a chance to visit them. It was coincidence that I was unable to do the Stone book but that the Sherrills could. It was coincidence that the mutual friend who brought Dave Wilkerson to John's office that day was the first person John had met who could speak in tongues. It was coincidence that Clement Stone was in New York that day.

It was the coincidence of having previously written books on missionary societies that I was given the Maryknoll assignment. It was a convenient coincidence that the Sherrills lived a few minutes away. It was the coincidence of my enthusiasm for Maryknoll that led me to urge the Sherrills to visit the place. It was the coincidence of having nothing to do on a Sunday afternoon with the kids home, that led the Sherrills to make their first visit to Maryknoll.

And now Maryknoll had moved in with the Sherrills.

And everybody was jabbering away in tongues.

I didn't know what to make of it.

But I realized I could no longer hold this subject at

arm's length. Though I did not want the Baptism for myself, I had to find out why everybody else was getting it.

I had to *know.*

I flew to Los Angeles on a Saturday afternoon because I wanted to be there for the Sunday services at Calvary Chapel. Len LeSourd had attended the services once and had returned to New York full of raves about the vigor and vitality of the congregation, all Jesus People. That Sunday morning, I went to Mass at the church around the corner from my hotel and then got lost on the labyrinth of California freeways as I tried to find Santa Ana and then Greenville Avenue and then the chapel. I knew that I was getting close when all the pedestrians I saw were carrying Bibles.

Calvary Chapel is at the end of Greenville Avenue. Beyond is farm land. The chapel is in California Spanish, and it is bigger than it looks from the outside. The facade on Greenville is actually the back of the chapel. Just a few years old, the chapel is already too small. In the foyer is an architect's rendering of how the size of the chapel, which seats seven hundred, is going to be doubled. As I approached the chapel, parked cars lined both sides of Greenville Avenue for three or four blocks. The neighborhood is middle-class, mostly small apartment buildings, clean, quiet, pretty. The Bible-carrying pedestrians I saw were casually dressed. Few of the men wore jackets. Some of the women wore ankle-length dresses. Although some of the adults were clearly grandparents, most of them were around thirty, and with small children strolling with them. Some of the teen-age boys had long hair or full hair, but not as many of them as I had expected, and I saw few beads. Some of the girls wore long dresses, but I saw no slacks and none of the hippie-type clothes I had associated with the Jesus People. I wondered if these people were heading for the same church I was, a church nationally identified with the Jesus Movement.

It was ten-twenty when I arrived at Calvary Chapel for the eleven o'clock service. The big parking lot was jammed and there was no space for two blocks in any direction. When I got back to the chapel and headed for the door off the parking lot, I came upon an outdoor patio where about three hundred people were sitting on folding chairs. Another fifty were standing about. The patio side of the chapel was comprised of glass sliding doors, which were open. The church was packed. The foyer was packed. A p.a. system was on, and I could hear Pastor Chuck Smith at his sermon. Everyone was listening intently. Since I knew I would be listening to the sermon myself in an hour, I used the time to study the people. If these, I thought, are Jesus People, then I have been grossly misled. I was expecting a Woodstock. I was looking at Smalltown, U.S.A. There was nothing to indicate that there was anything unusual, anything different, about these people. They could have been a Protestant congregation anywhere in the country. I found myself feeling a little disappointed.

The sermon ended. Pastor Smith began the closing prayer. Everybody in the chapel and on the patio stood and bowed their heads. Then there was a hymn. I couldn't believe the singing. It was full and vigorous and confident. People looked at each other and smiled. I thought of the singing we had done at Mass that morning, so timid, so inhibited, as it usually was at Mass anywhere—Catholics still hadn't gotten the hang of it. I thought, too, of the singing at other Protestant services I had attended, with a good choir to make up for any lack of congregation participation. This crowd was different. They were with it. They sang out. The air rang with a sense of freedom and joy, and I was moved.

The service ended, and there was an immediate traffic jam of people leaving the chapel and others entering. I went in and found a seat. Within minutes, the chapel was packed, the foyer was packed, the patio was packed, and with the same type of people as before. On my right was a young man with blond hair down to his shoulders, which was what I expected, but on my left was a matronly woman, small, trim, gray, a grandmother, and I had not expected that. Many people seemed to know each other and there was a good deal of conversation, something else a Catholic can't get used to in church. I saw a note in the chapel bulletin: "The Service of Worship begins with the first note of the organ. From there, let us cease all conversation with others and talk with God. If you must whisper—whisper a prayer." I wondered why the admonition was necessary.

Promptly at eleven, the organ began, and people settled down. The service began with several hymns, and again the singing was amazing. I was prepared not to know the hymns; and since I cannot read music I did not reach for a hymnal each time we were told to stand and sing. The grandmother on my left noticed this and, on each hymn, she moved close to me and extended her hymnal, sharing it. I tried to fake it, timid, inhibited, preferring to listen. One hymn had a counter-melody which the girls sang, and the whole thing came off as well as a carefully rehearsed choral group.

Pastor Chuck Smith appeared to be around forty. Balding, he was well-built, and his heavy shoulders gave him the impression of being taller than he is. He spoke firmly, moderately, with none of the fire-and-brimstone I expected. From time to time, he stopped, looked afar, and softly said: "Praise the Lord." From time to time, there seemed to be tears in his eyes. He did not gesture much. His sermon that morning was called "The Perils of Unbelief," and his primary example was Zacharias, the father of John the Baptist, who was struck dumb when he didn't believe the angel who told him he was going to become a father in his old age. "Do what God tells you," Smith said in his sermon. "Unbelief can rob you of the joys and thrills that God has in store for you." Doubt arose, he said, when people tried to make decisions based only on their natural senses. "Listen to the Lord," Smith said. "He's talking to you all the time." This, I learned as I went along, is the general conviction of the Jesus People.

When Smith finished his sermon, four children, three of them infants, were brought to him by their parents for what he called "dedication." In a way, it was a baptism ceremony, perhaps more of a presentation ceremony. After joking amiably with the parents, Smith took each child into his arms and prayed, each time a little differently, that the child would be filled with the Holy Spirit and would grow up in the love of the Lord. It was a very touching thing to watch, especially when one baby cried as he was returned to his parents and stopped only after he was retrieved briefly by Smith.

Then Smith went back to the lectern and asked us to rise for the benediction. As soon as he began to pray, a distinct change occurred in the church. I sensed a sudden tension. A rustling began all around me and I looked about to see what it was. The people were praying along with Smith. I could hear several of them whispering rapidly: "Jesus, Jesus, Jesus, Jeeesus!" Here and there, people, old and young, had their arms outstretched, and they were swaying slightly. I heard a familiar sound and turned. A boy, perhaps fifteen, was speaking in tongues as he pressed his Bible to his chest. Next to him was a man with tears streaming from his closed eyes as his mouth moved soundlessly. All this went on for only two or three minutes, until Smith pronounced a sharp "Amen!" and then the people returned to the way they had been, as though they were snapping out of something. The closing hymn was rousing.

As I left, I found myself being funneled onto a line that led to Chuck Smith, standing at the door shaking hands. He knew a lot of people by name, and they addressed him by his first name. Again, he seemed to have tears in his eyes. With the young, Smith shook hands in a different way, each grabbing the other by the thumb and then bringing up forearms back to back. When I got to Smith, we shook hands straight. I only had time to ask him: "May I call you for an appointment?" He nodded, but he was already grabbing the thumb of someone behind me. Outside, everybody was grabbing thumbs.

That evening, I went out to the Sunset Strip where, according to what I had read and been told, throngs of Jesus People gathered every night to witness—to tell others how the Lord had changed their lives, this being an effort to make conversions. But no one was there. It was around nine, and I wondered if I were too early or too late. I got out of the car and walked a few blocks, looking for coffeehouses. Nothing. So I drove to a gas station and asked the attendant: "Where are all the Jesus People tonight?"

"Where they're supposed to be," he said. "It's Sunday. They're in church."

2

Right On!

Monday morning I called the *Hollywood Free Paper* and was told that Jesus loves me.

Duane Pederson is probably the best known of the Jesus People leaders, and one reason for this is that the newspaper he edits—and in which his picture often appears—has a national circulation of over five hundred thousand. Because he is known widely, Pederson travels more than other leaders I met, attending campus rallies and appearing on programs with other leaders. It was Pederson, in fact, who coined the expression "Jesus People" after getting tired of hearing members in the movement referred to as Jesus Freaks. When I met him, he admitted to being over thirty. Tall, blond, well-built, good looking, he was a bachelor. As a boy, he wanted to go into show business, despite the fact that he had a severe stammer. He doesn't have it any longer. He is a calm man, speaks slowly, and he has a biting sense of humor, aimed mostly at the clergy and churches.

Duane Pederson was born on a farm near Hastings, Minnesota. Because of his stammer, he was a loner in his boyhood. In high school, he rarely asked a girl for a date because he knew how difficult it would be for him to keep a conversation going. In college, he withdrew even more into himself. And yet he had this urge to perform. In his youth, he once bought a couple of books on sleight of hand and turned himself into a good magician. He was always ready to perform, as long as he didn't have to speak; and because he didn't speak much in the first place, there weren't many people who found out how good he was. In college, he heard that the drama club was about to cast a play. Determined to get out of his shell, he got a copy of the play and memorized the leading part. When he walked into the audition and announced that he wanted to try out for the lead, his friends laughed. He got the part, and it wasn't until later that the director found out about his stammer.

After college, Pederson managed to get his magic act booked into some of the smaller nightclubs in the Northwest. As his confidence grew, he added some well-rehearsed patter, and he started getting better jobs. The top booking agents for the area were in Los Angeles; Pederson moved there in order to have contact with the agents and get top bookings. He found out he could sing, and so, besides his own act, he got bookings with vocal groups. He should have been happy, but he was not. Traveling so much, leading a topsy-turvy life, constantly under pressure, Pederson began to drink heavily. And he went on drugs. He knew this couldn't go on much longer, but he didn't know how to stop it.

Several years ago, Pederson was working in a Minneapolis club when he was unexpectedly visited one night by a California friend he had not seen for a while. The friend said he had quit show business, and Pederson took this as the reason for the change in the man: he looked rested and refreshed, vital and vigorous. They agreed to have lunch the next day. At lunch, the man explained what had really happened to him: he had quit drinking and drugs and promiscuity, and he had given his life to Jesus Christ.

He said: "Duane, I've never been happier. I've never been a better man."

Pederson said: "Well, if religion is what changed you, maybe I can use some of it myself. I sure don't like the life I'm leading."

"You can change," the man said. "All you've got to do is ask Jesus to take over your life. Go ahead."

"Now?"

"Why not?"

There, in a downtown Minneapolis restaurant, Duane Pederson bowed his head and really prayed for the first time in his life. When he looked up, he was a different man. For one thing, he never stammered again. For another, he quit liquor and drugs.

He wanted to *do* something about it. He joined a church and quickly became a very active member. However, he gradually became aware that most of the people who attended the church regarded it as a private club. They felt secure in their faith and were financially secure in their lives, and they didn't want to associate with any other kind of people. Their religion didn't seem to be doing anything for them at all. Pederson felt that religion was meant for people like himself—the gypsies, the people with problems, the down-and-outers. From his Bible, he learned that these were the kinds of people Jesus attracted—thieves, prostitutes, adulterers, and he solved their problems. Pederson began rounding up Minneapolis gypsies and taking them to the church services, hoping they would accept Christ as their Lord and become whole again.

One day the pastor took Pederson aside and said: "Duane, some members of the congregation are complaining about the people you are bringing here. I know you mean well, but this place is not a Skid Row mission. I'll have to ask you to stop it."

Pederson stopped it. He stopped going to the church himself. But he could not put a stop to the urge he felt to reach out to the desperate gypsies who did not know as yet what the Lord could do for them. He remembered the countless gypsies he had seen in California, loitering along the Strip and Hollywood Boulevard, kids most of them, many of them addicts and winos and prostitutes, male and female, kids from all over the country, crashing in filthy pads, sleeping outdoors, stealing to survive, kids looking in the wrong places for a peace they would never find, heading for an early grave. Pederson found himself thinking about the California gypsies so much that he wondered if the Lord wanted him to go to California to work among the kids. He decided to put out a fleece, as Gideon did in the Bible. God told Gideon to step forward and become the leader of his people, but Gideon, who had a low opinion of himself, couldn't believe that God would choose him for such an important job, so he asked God for a sign. He said he would put a fleece on the floor of his barn and if, in the morning, the floor was wet but the fleece was dry, he would know that God had truly spoken to him. In the morning, the floor was wet and the fleece was dry. Still unsure, Gideon told God that if, the next morning, the floor was dry but the fleece was wet, he would have no more doubts. Next morning, the floor was dry and the fleece was wet. Gideon stepped forward. In his prayers, Duane Pederson told God that he would go to California to work with the gypsies and he would know that he was doing what God wanted him to do if he found a church that would accept the kids.

In California, Duane Pederson had no trouble making contact with the kids. They were everywhere. He talked to many of them and he was able to lead some of them to

Christ. But church after church turned them down, and so they had no place to worship, no place to study, no place where they could get off the streets, where they could escape the temptations that threatened them. It was out of this that Pederson decided to become a minister himself and open his own church for the gypsies. He entered a Bible college in Missouri.

It did not take him long to find out that his fellow students knew next to nothing about the world and wanted no part of it. Insulated by their suburbanite mentalities, they felt that Pederson's concern for street people made him some kind of a fanatic. All they wanted for themselves was an appointment to a nice church in a nice neighborhood with a nice congregation and a nice family of their own. Pederson learned about their prudishness when he went swimming at the city pool one day and happened to mention it when he got back to school. He was immediately reprimanded: he had gone swimming in a mixed pool. He said he hadn't noticed any blacks there and that, in the first place, he thought discrimination was immoral. The complaint was clarified: he, a seminarian, had gone to a pool where males and females were allowed to swim together. He shook his head over that.

He had noticed that the town's young people gathered on street corners every evening, rapping and flirting with trouble, so he made a tour of the nearby churches, offering to supervise a youth center if the church provided the space. He got no takers, so he opened a teen club of his own, equipping it with furniture, a juke box, refreshment machines and some pool tables he had been able to scrounge. He began spending so much time at the club that his studies suffered. Examination time was coming, and he knew he was not prepared. Then he heard that some upperclassmen had made a list of the answers to the exam and were selling it to his classmates, and he bought a copy.

Unexpectedly, he suffered a severe blow. Some people of the town, including members of the faculty, had compiled a petition which they presented to the town government, asking that the teen club be closed for being an improper place for young people to gather. It was closed.

In this mood, Duane Pederson took the exam. Two days later, he was summoned before a faculty committee. Apparently, some of the answers on the list were wrong, and the pattern of errors by students who used the list was too obvious for the faculty to overlook. Pederson was asked if he had cheated on the test. He said yes. He was told to apologize to the committee. He did so. He was asked to name those who had been involved. When he refused, he was thrown out of the school, and as far as he knew he was the only student to be expelled for cheating.

That did it. Duane Pederson wanted no more to do with Christians. Despite the personal happiness his conversion had brought him, it had also brought him nothing but trouble with Christians wherever he went. He decided that if this was the way Christians treated each other, he would forget the whole thing. He returned to Hollywood and got a job on a television series for children which was then in the planning stage.

But that gnawing persisted inside him. Evening after evening, sometimes against his own will, he found himself out on the Strip, rapping with the hippies about Jesus Christ. He was there one night when several people came down the street distributing underground newspapers. He accepted a few and saw that they all advocated political revolutions and sexual revolutions. Most of the ads were about coffee houses where he knew drugs could easily be obtained.

As he stood there, paging through the papers, the thought entered his mind: "There isn't a single Christian newspaper for these kids."

In that same instant, he knew what the Lord wanted him to do.

He was to start a Christian newspaper and see to it that it got into the hands of the gypsies—all gypsies from coast to coast.

The realization shot through him the same sense of relief that he had experienced that day in the Minneapolis restaurant when he submitted himself to Jesus Christ. He knew it was the right thing to do.

He happened to be broke. This did not bother him. Next day, he began making a tour of his friends for donations to start the paper. Some friends thought he was crazy and gave him nothing. Most friends gave him five or ten dollars. Some gave as much as fifty. One friend, as a result of the discussion about the newspaper, gave himself to Christ.

There was already a popular and radical underground publication called the *Los Angeles Free Paper.* Duane Pederson called his the *Hollywood Free Paper.* A tabloid, light on copy and heavy on psychedelic art, the message of the paper was: *Jesus is where it's at. Come and talk to us about it.* Pederson wrote the first edition himself and had ten thousand copies printed. He also distributed the first edition himself—on the Strip, along Hollywood Boulevard, up and down Vine, at Pershing Square, on the beaches, wherever the gypsies were, and he popped the paper into cars waiting at traffic lights. Some people paid him on the spot—a nickel, a dime, a quarter. Others took the paper home and read it, and sent him some folding money. Mail drawn by the first edition indicated that, as a result of it, six hundred people had taken Christ into their lives.

When I met Duane Pederson, the paper was finishing its third year. Besides being distributed in Southern California, plates were being flown to fourteen other cities for printing and distribution by local Jesus People. Pederson has registered the expression "Jesus People," he has a board of directors, he has an accounting firm, and his books are open to anyone who wants to see them. In California, a religious organization like Pederson's has the right to ordain ministers. Pederson considers himself ordained; he has ordained others.

When I met him, Pederson's office and home were in a small frame house on Fountain Street. The place was Spartan. The furniture was plain and old. There were no carpets. On the door was a sign: "Please Come In—We are expecting you." In what used to be a living room, a receptionist sat at a small desk, typing labels and taking phone calls, always greeting the caller with the news that

Jesus loved him. At the far end of the room, a young Oriental sorted papers on a table. Pederson was out, and I was invited to sit on an ancient sofa, occupied at the moment by a small dog of unidentifiable lineage who did not move when I joined him. The walls were lined with posters relevant to the movement, some of them saying: "Jesus Is Coming" and "Jesus Is My Bag" and "I love you. . . . if that's okay. (signed) Jesus Christ." On shelves in a wall were many New Testaments, copies of the newspaper, boxes of bumper stickers ("Honk if you love Jesus" and "I am high on the love of my Jesus") and boxes of lapel buttons bearing similar messages.

Duane Pederson arrived and we went into his office, which appeared to have been a bedroom. His desk was big and old, cluttered with mail and publications. His phone had four or five push buttons which flickered frequently as we talked, but he did not take any calls. The room was sparsely furnished. Pederson had on worn dark slacks, a dark sweater and boots. His blond hair was moderately full and long. He used to have a beard but he didn't at the moment. He looked like Billy Graham loafing around the house on a day off.

As he told me about himself, Pederson would at times look away and smile sadly whenever he referred to his problems with ministers and churches. At one point he said: "I believe that the main thing in the Jesus movement is the acceptance by all Christians, whether charismatic or not, that they must regard each other as members of the Body of Christ—all brothers and sisters in the Lord, and that they cannot be divided, as they once were and still are, by churches." Pederson said he believed that the ecumenical trend in the Christian world would ultimately be brought to fulfillment from the grass roots, by the Jesus People, and not as a result of any theological or authoritarian compromises at the top.

I asked Pederson if the Jesus People had a credo, and he answered: "Accept Jesus Christ as the son of God, accept his deity, accept his love, and then you can accept yourself. Then when you pray to Jesus Christ for help, you know you will get it because you are praying to God and not some human being who lived two thousand years ago."

I asked: "Are you suggesting that the thousands of kids who have become Jesus People had never before in their lives heard that Jesus Christ is the son of God?"

"Oh, they heard it," Pederson said, "and most of them heard it at an age when they could have believed it and lived it without any problems. But then they got older and they saw what adult Christians were doing to the world, and they decided that if Jesus Christ was the son of God or not didn't make much difference. Nobody was living as he said they should. So they turned off and dropped out. But they're believing it and living it now because they're hearing it from kids their own age and they're seeing for themselves what Jesus can do to a life."

I asked Pederson if he had received the Baptism in the Holy Spirit, and he said yes. I asked if he had received any of the gifts of the Spirit, and he said yes. Then I could tell by the look on his face that he did not want to pursue this subject any further, which was something that happened with all of the Jesus People leaders I interviewed across the country. So I asked him what evidence was most convincing to him that the Holy Spirit was in the Jesus People Movement. I expected him to say tongues.

"The Movement itself," he said. "It's not an accident. It isn't a phenomenon. It's not just a fad. The whole thing is predicted in the Bible. Before the Second Coming of Christ, there would be certain wars and Depressions. The kids would leave home and hit the road. There would be a surge of homosexuality. The nation of Israel would rise again. The countries of Europe would unite. The Holy Spirit would touch millions of lives. The Anti-Christ would appear. The Christians would be persecuted, and there would be the final war, brought to an end by the return of Christ. Then we'll have a thousand years of peace, until Judgment Day and the end of the world."

I asked: "When is all this going to happen?"

"It's going on right now," he said. "Read the papers. Read the Bible."

"I will," I said. "Now, tell me, what lasting good do you think the Movement is achieving?"

"First," he said, "thousands of kids are now living truly Christian lives. You see, we have been living in a career-oriented society. Parents push their kids hard at school so they'll be at the head of their class. When he gets out into the world, he is pressured to succeed fast just for the sake of success. He has to prove that his parents raised him right. So he gets caught up in all the pressures and tensions and dishonesty and hypocrisy of the world his parents inherited from their parents. At thirty, he may be rich and successful, but he is miserable. He has his psychiatrist, he has a mistress, he may have a boy friend, and he drinks too much. He can't communicate with the people closest to him because he can't let them know what kind of life he's leading. He has to keep fighting fiercely to survive. When he loses, he has nothing to fall back on, and he cracks up.

"Well, today's kids have taken a look at the world they have inherited, and they don't like it. They know that you don't have to be rich to be happy, and that, in fact, the less you have the happier you can be because you have less to worry about. Today's kids aren't interested in things. They are not interested in status. They are interested in values and principles. They want to change the world. For a while, they tried to change the world by joining radical movements and using violence and destruction. Well, that didn't change much, did it? Then a lot of them just dropped out, became hippies, turning on with drugs and sex and booze. So a lot of them started to die young.

"Now today's kids are thinking. They're reading. They're rapping. They have found out that Christianity today is nowhere near the kind of life that Jesus Christ said it could be and should be, a life of peace and brotherhood and love, with everybody sharing. This is the world they want. But they have also found out that before they can change the world they have to change themselves, and the first step in doing that is making a total commitment of your life to Christ. After that, he takes over. That's why we put out the paper, to let kids know that. That's why we put on the rock festivals—we've filled the Hollywood Palladium, even the Hollywood Bowl, to get a lot of kids together to hear the music, and then we witness to them about what the Lord has done in our own lives and what he can do in theirs. Everytime, hundreds come forward to the stage to make their commitments.

"They don't have to join communes, although that's all right. When you're young in the faith it makes sense to live with people who are stronger and can help you mature. But I can drive you around town and introduce you to a hundred families that appear to be straight and seem to be living 'normal' lives, but you hang around for a couple of hours and see how they treat each other and their neighbors. Listen to what they talk about—the Lord. These people are bound to have a good effect on the community. And I believe it's lasting.

"Another lasting good, I think," Pederson went on, "is the fact that thousands of drug addicts are kicking their habits when they make the commitment. About eighty-five percent of the Jesus People either were addicts or were well on their way to becoming addicts. Now, there is no such thing as a happy addict. The longer a person is hooked, the heavier his habit becomes, and the more it is going to cost him every day. If he can't get the money legitimately, he is going to have to steal or become a prostitute. He knows that if he can't get a fix when he needs one, he will go into withdrawal. This is a hell and it can kill him. All addicts want to change, but they think they can't. By witnessing to addicts about their own lives, the Jesus People can prove that change is certain if the addict will give his life to Christ.

"What happens next is miraculous. The committed addict goes through a sixty-second withdrawal. It doesn't make any difference how long he's been an addict or how heavy his habit was, he is cured in sixty seconds. I've seen it happen hundreds of times. I was watching one kid as he made his commitment: the tracks on his arm dried up and fell off, like old scabs. In sixty seconds.

"Another boy came in here one morning with a wonderful story. He had gone out to the beach the night before to have a little party by himself. He took an overdose. He lay there for five hours, slowly dying, and he knew what was happening to him. He needed help, but he couldn't move and nobody came near him. He felt himself slipping out, and in his mind he cried, 'Jesus, help me! Jesus, take over or I'm sunk. Jesus, let me live for you!' He kept sinking into the darkness, and he was sure this was death. He blacked out. A few hours later, he awoke in the sun. He was exhausted, but he was alive. He remembered his prayer and he knew that he meant it. He came back into town and came over here and told us what happened. Then he said, 'Okay, what do I do next?' He's still clean, and he's one of our best workers.

"Another time, I gave a talk to a Kiwanis club out of town, and after it a man came up to me and asked if I could help his son. The kid was an addict. I told him to bring the boy to my hotel and leave us alone. He did. I started to talk to the boy about the Lord, but I could see he wasn't interested. He was bored, and he was wondering when he was going to get out of there so that he could take another fix. I was determined that the kid wouldn't leave until he had given his life to Jesus Christ or went into withdrawal. I kept talking, telling him how Jesus could help him, how the Lord could straighten him out. He wasn't listening. Every time he got up to head for the door, I pushed him back in the chair.

"After a couple of hours, he started sweating. Then he got the chills. He knew what was starting and he was scared. He began begging me to let him leave. I kept talking, telling him what Jesus had done for other kids I knew, what he had done for me. I showed him passages of the Bible where Jesus repeatedly promised to help those who asked, those who gave their lives to him. He wouldn't look; he wouldn't listen. In the middle of the night, he got so sick that I had to put him to bed, fully clothed, and cover him up and hold him down. I kept talking.

"It was morning before the boy finally said, 'Okay, Duane, okay. I believe you. I'll say it. I'll do it. Oh, Jesus, Jesus, my savior, help me. I'm a sinner. I want to change. Help me. Save me.' Fifteen minutes later, we were walking up the street to a restaurant where we could get an early breakfast. The boy was carrying a Bible I had given him. We had called his father, and the man was driving in to join me and his son. His new son."

Pederson smiled a little and looked away. He said: "The general attitude is that the best treatment for drug addiction is the Synanon program—substitute drugs and group therapy. They have a cure-rate of ten or eleven percent. As you know, a lot of the guys coming home from Vietnam are hooked on drugs, and the military is trying to find some way to help them. Recently some people from the Pentagon were out here. They were trying to find out how come Synanon has only a ten or eleven percent cure-rate and Jesus Christ has a hundred." He laughed.

I asked: "When a person makes the commitment that turns him into Jesus People, does he experience the Baptism in the Holy Spirit?"

Pederson said: "Most of the time."

"Right away?"

"Most of the time."

"And does he speak in tongues?"

"Most of the time."

"Right away?"

"Most of the time. Some acquire it later on."

"Besides tongues, have you witnessed any of the other gifts of the Spirit?"

"I've witnessed them all."

He was so matter of fact about it. All the Jesus People turned out to be that way. Besides tongues, the gifts were interpretation of tongues, wisdom, knowledge, faith, healing, performing miracles, prophecy and the discerning of spirits. That's quite a list of spiritual faculties to have witnessed. So I nodded at Duane Pederson, and we went on.

Duane Pederson feels that a disturbing characteristic prevalent in today's young people is that they are so transient, literally and figuratively. Literally, they all have transportation—a car, a motorbike—or they can get it. And they all have thumbs. Thousands of parents know that when a kid decides to hit the road the only way to stop him is to put him in chains. Today's kids want to move around. Figuratively, the kids are on the loose because they have rejected their parents' moral and social standards without replacing them with anything but whims of the moment. Pederson said: "Today's kids are better educated, not just academically, but they learn fast on the streets, and that's where they run into trouble."

But Pederson believes there is an answer to the problem: the Movement. As the circulation of the *Hollywood Free Paper* shows, there are Jesus People all over the country. If they are more abundantly noticeable in California, it is because the weather allows them to go outdoors more. Also, most of the pioneers of the Movement are in California, as are most of the more colorful leaders. What is lacking in many parts of the country is this kind of experienced leadership. Since the effects of the Baptism in the Holy Spirit can fade if they are not strengthened by an increased spiritual life, here and there across the country pockets of Jesus People have risen and fallen. Duane Pederson is working to prevent the fade-outs by conducting leadership seminars for representatives of these groups early in their development. The sessions are held in the summer in Hollywood, they last a week, and they include courses in how to conduct a prayer meeting, how to teach Bible studies and how to street-witness. If travel costs are prohibitive for distant groups, Pederson is ready to take his team of instructors to a central point in that area. He is convinced that by producing a network of strong leaders across the country, the Movement can be assured of a steady and expanding growth. As a result, when the young transients start getting itchy feet and hit the road, it will practically be impossible for them to travel more than a few miles in any given direction without running into some Jesus People who will be able to help them get their heads straight.

I said: "You sound as though the Movement is here to stay."

He laughed. "Read the papers. Read your Bible."

Barry Wood was the pastor of the First Baptist Church of Beverly Hills. This sounded like a swanky job, but it turned out not to be. The church was located in a middle-class neighborhood; the streets were lined with modest frame homes, most of them old, and many of the lawns needed tending. The parked cars I saw were low-priced. In mid-afternoon, there was no one about.

Wood, a Texan, was casually dressed, not because this was California but because, as with Pederson, this was the uniform of the Movement. I stopped wearing ties and suits myself so that I wouldn't seem too much of an outlander.

Wood had spent his earlier ministry as an evangelist, mostly along the Bible Belt, and he became well known. But he was not a happy man. Each time he'd return to a town, he would notice that there were fewer young people at the services. Young people he met as he traveled all seemed to be going beatnik. Some of them confided to him that they were on drugs. He could see for himself that some of them drank. He was appalled by the casual attitude among the young toward pregnancies out of wedlock. His job, as a minister, was to lead people in the opposite moral direction, and he began to wonder just how successful he was after all. He talked to parents. They told him they couldn't do anything with their kids. When he asked them what they were trying to do, he found out that they weren't really trying at all. This lethargy among adult Christians weighed on him like a mountain. He didn't know what to do about his work. He didn't know what to do about himself.

"I was an empty man," he told me, his voice sad. "I realized I was making Christianity a career, when I should have been making it a way of life for people. Even realizing this didn't help because I still didn't know what to do about it. To attract teen-agers, I tried using rock music at a couple of services. The adults brought the roof down on my head. After that, pastors would ask me about the rock music before signing me up to preach at revivals. I had to drop it because the Establishment didn't like it. It didn't take me long to become a very anti-Establishment member of the Establishment."

Then he began to hear about the growing national interest in the Holy Spirit, and he began to read books about the Spirit, including John Sherrill's. "It was amazing," he said. "Here I was, seminary-trained, and I knew next to nothing about the Holy Spirit, except that the Pentecostals carried on a lot about him. But from my reading I learned that all sorts of people were now carrying on about the Holy Spirit, people of all denominations, including my own. My spiritual life had become so arid. I knew I needed something; and if the Baptism was it, then I wanted it. I started to pray for it."

I asked: "Did you receive it?"

"In January, 1968, when I was twenty-nine."

"Did you receive tongues?"

He shook his head. "Not then; but I was filled with a sense of joy, of sweetness, and I acquired a great love for people. I knew that God had something special in store for me. I knew that one day the Holy Spirit would lead me to it. I just prayed and prayed that God would put me somewhere with the kids."

Early in 1969, Wood received the information that the First Baptist Church of Beverly Hills, California, was seeking a new pastor, and the congregation invited him to come out and conduct services, then hang around for a few days as he and they sized each other up. The First Baptist Church of Beverly Hills was located just a few blocks off Sunset Strip. Wood accepted the invitation. He conducted services. He hung around for a few days. One evening he went for a walk. And he discovered the Strip, mobbed with hippies, part-time hippies, hippie-watchers and hippie-exploiters.

He knew he was home.

He was offered the job at First Baptist. He accepted it. And First Baptist would never be the same.

Already working on the Strip was Arthur Blessitt, also an ordained Baptist minister in the same age group. Blessitt was from Mississippi, where he was ordained and subsequently began his ministry. He also served in Montana and was a circuit rider in the Southwest. Then he and his wife went to San Francisco, where Blessitt intended to further his education. But he spent more evenings with the hippies at North Beach than he did over his books. He came to the conclusion that the Lord wanted him to work with the hippies, so he and his wife moved to Beverly Hills where they found an apartment near the Strip.

Blessitt supported himself as a visiting preacher to numerous Southern California churches, but he spent his evenings on the Strip, rapping with the hippies about the Lord. This was the era of coffeehouses, where more drugs were sold than coffee. Having Blessitt in the place, talking about the Lord, slowed down the sales of coffee as well as of drugs, and owners started putting him out, sometimes calling the police for help to do so. Now and then, this brought on a riot by the hippies who wanted to hear Blessitt, and Blessitt began to get into the papers.

Blessitt knew the owner of a go-go bar on the Strip. Knowing that business was slow in the middle of the week, Blessitt asked the man if he could use the place for a witnessing service on a Tuesday night. The man thought Blessitt was crazy and told him so, but Blessitt persisted and the man finally agreed. The place was packed that night, as it was for the next six Tuesdays. Again, Blessitt got into the papers. As a result, CBS television did about twenty minutes locally on Blessitt's project, and he got about five minutes on the network. Suddenly Arthur Blessitt was a national celebrity. In came a flood of offers from night clubs across the country at thousands of dollars. He was offered his own radio show, his own television show. But he knew that these people weren't interested in hearing him preach the Gospel; they just wanted a Jesus freak to do his act. Blessitt turned everybody down.

He realized, however, that, as important as his street witnessing was, having a place where the kids could gather indoors would give his work a more solid foundation. He found such a place, a two-story building at 9109 Sunset, and he planned on using the first floor as something of a rap room and the second floor as a prayer room. Without any idea of where the money was going to come from, he signed a five-year lease at six hundred dollars a month. Actually, he had an idea of the only place the money could come from: God. Blessitt called the project His Place.

From the start, His Place was a smash. Every night, kids packed the rap room. Gradually they began to go upstairs to pray. But these were kids off the streets, and many of them brought in the problems of the streets. Before the first week was out, Blessitt had to put this sign on the door:

1. No dope.
2. No alcohol.
3. No hassling.
4. No crashing.
5. No making out.
6. No guns, knives, or chains.

Violators will be banned for thirty days.

Hundreds of kids were drifting in and out of His Place far into the night; and since it was impossible to frisk each one, some drugs got in. Arthur Blessitt had a way of curbing this. As soon as an addict committed his life to Christ, he was led into the john and required to empty his pockets. Any dope he had on him went into the toilet. Then the new Christian was led upstairs to pray.

Blessitt's serious trouble did not come from the kids. It came from his neighbors on the Strip, the owners of go-go joints, strip joints, make-out bars, gay bars and the coffeehouses where drug sales were openly made. As more and more of the kids hung around His Place, business dropped off badly at the other spots, and the owners began to complain. Harassment started. On weekends, when the quasi-hippies from Pasadena arrived in their Cadillacs, they could break every traffic law on the books and not be bothered; but let a hippie-looking Jesus Person set foot off the curb before the light was green and he got busted. If some smart guys from anywhere decided to break up some street-witnessing near His Place, it was the Jesus People who got clubbed by the riot squads. Frequently the police invaded His Place, accusing Blessitt of harboring runaways and draft dodgers or having drugs on the premises. Everybody would be searched and required to produce identification. Sometimes gangs of motorbikers would come and try to wreck the place. One night somebody put LSD in the Kool-Aid, and everybody went on an unexpected trip.

Arthur Blessitt himself was arrested three times, for blocking pedestrian traffic with his witnessing groups. Each time he was acquitted. One night he led a couple of hundred Jesus People in a token protest demonstration at police headquarters. And he told the sheriff's office that he could gather several thousand protestors, if this was what was needed to make his point. Blessitt looked upon His Place as a church, and he believed that the frequent invasions by police without warrants were an infringement of the freedom of religion. The invasions ended.

When the lease on His Place expired, the landlord refused to renew it. Blessitt began to look for another spot on the Strip, and there were several vacancies—joints that had gone out of business because the kids weren't going there anymore. But when the owners saw that it was Blessitt who wanted the place, they told him it was not for rent, despite the sign on the door. To get around this, Blessitt had a friend make the inquiry on a vacancy in the next block. It had been a strip joint, and the landlord got the impression that it was going to be a strip joint again. He granted the lease. Later, when he drove by and discovered that his bar was the new His Place, he went into court, charging that the lease had been broken because Blessitt was using the bar for reasons not stipulated in the lease. The court decided in favor of the landlord; but as the judge was ordering Arthur Blessitt to vacate the premises in a week, he added that he was sorry to do this because he knew of the good work Blessitt was doing there. That looked like the end of His Place. Arthur Blessitt turned to the only person he could. He turned to the Lord.

In His Place was a large cross. The day after receiving the eviction notice, Blessitt had the cross taken outside. He mounted the cross and had himself chained to it. This was not a protest. It was a prayer. And Arthur Blessitt vowed that he would remain on the cross, fasting, until the Lord provided a new location for His place.

Again Blessitt was in the papers. Again the television crews arrived. Telegrams and letters arrived from all over the world, all of them encouraging, all promising prayers. Far into the night, great crowds gathered around the cross, encouraging, praying. Heavy traffic moved by slowly, people staring, people calling out: "Right on!" Many people committed their lives to Christ at the foot of that cross. Arrangements had previously been made for Blessitt to marry a Jesus People couple; now he married them from the cross. Every few days, some friend would come running with a lead on a new location, but then the lead would fizzle out. Blessitt remained on the cross. Every day, his wife would bring their three children to visit him. Nobody criticized Blessitt for what he was doing. Nobody said he was wasting his time. Nobody said he was being a fool. People knew that this was something he had to do, and this was the only way he could do it. And all the time, across the street and a short distance off, there was a squad car, night and day, the police watching but not approaching.

Blessitt remained on the cross four weeks. Then a lead materialized. Down the street were two adjacent buildings, former nightclubs, and the owner was willing to rent them to Blessitt on an unbreakable lease. The owner later told Blessitt that when the news of the lease got out, his insurance was cancelled and neighbors telephoned and wrote him their complaints. But the man did not care. He knew he was doing the right thing. Arthur Blessitt came down from the cross.

I did not meet Arthur Blessitt. He had gradually become aware that the Lord wanted him to go to Europe and minister to the thousands of young American gypsies who had migrated there and were becoming the same public problem there with drugs that they had been at home. Then, when he learned that the buildings of the third His Place were to be demolished, he accepted this as further guidance, and he went to Europe.

Barry Wood met Arthur Blessitt early in his own street

ministry on the Strip, and they became good friends. Wood was with Blessitt on the token protest at police headquarters that night. Also, because no crashing was allowed at His Place, Wood let the newly converted boys and young men crash in the First Baptist Church of Beverly Hills.

"I had to," he told me. "There was no other safe place. This is a highly homosexual neighborhood. I'm surrounded by homosexuals. They go up to the Strip at night and invite the runaways and young hippies to crash at their place. Well, a new Christian who is young in the faith might not have the strength to say no, so we felt they'd be safer in the church. Since then, we've bought the two homes behind the church, and the guys stay there. I think there are fifteen or sixteen there now, but we've had as high as forty. They stay various lengths of time, usually until they feel confident about their judgment and get a job and can find a place to live among other Christians."

To Jesus People, a Christian is anyone who has had his "experience with the Lord," which means receiving the Baptism of the Holy Spirits and its gifts. If, by his circumstances, an individual is obviously in the Jesus Movement, he thinks it is odd of you to ask if he has received the Baptism and its gifts. His answer is usually an appraising stare and maybe a nod. On the whole trip, nobody asked me if I'd had the Baptism. I had a straight haircut; I usually wore a tie and a jacket; I didn't speak the hippie lingo, and I often had to ask for translations when it was spoken to me. Only once was I challenged to join a group, and only then because the outfit needed a writer. This "in" attitude among so many of the Jesus People has been the cause of criticism by some observers of the Movement. Others who have been baptized only by water are made to feel like lesser Christians. I found this to be true to some extent, but the more I ran into it the more I was able to understand it. Instead of spiritual pride, it was, in most cases, a pride in a newly found spirituality, as though to say: "Unless you have been down at the bottom of life's barrel for a while, you will never be able to understand what it is like to find yourself suddenly up into the clean air." The fact that Jesus People do street-witnessing is evidence that they seek to share the joys of the Baptism with others. Even so, it seemed to me that they appeared to concentrate their efforts mostly on others who looked like good prospects: their own kind.

When Barry Wood took the pulpit of First Baptist, he had a congregation of about two hundred straights. As his street work progressed, he invited his newly converted Jesus People to attend his church services. The straights began to object; they also objected to the rock music Wood gradually introduced. Wood told them that as long as he was pastor of the church he would do things his way and if they didn't like it they could fire him. Instead of firing him, the straights drifted away until only a handful remained. Today the congregation numbers around three hundred, most of them Jesus People. Wood said: "These days, there is more joy in ten minutes at our services than there was in the history of the church."

Like Arthur Blessitt, Barry Wood was put out of many of the coffeehouses and nightclubs on the Strip in his early days. He told me: "I decided that if people wouldn't let me witness in their nightclubs, I'd open one of my own." And he did—the *Right On!,* on the Strip. Wood told me that it was impossible to get into the place on weekends, that there was a lot of rapping about Jesus among the audience and a lot of witnessing from the stage. I must have gone there on an off night. It was Friday; there were about fifty people in the audience, most of them men, many over thirty. There was a bar but no alcoholic beverages were sold, of course, and I didn't see any ash trays. The show was comprised of a white group that did country music and a black group that did soul. I don't have an ear for either type of music, and so I was unable to judge whether the groups were good. Also, I was unable to understand most of the lyrics, and so I was unable to determine where the songs were of a religious nature. Two performers—a white boy and a black girl—witnessed briefly and, I thought, uncomfortably. There was no reaction from the audience. Before and after the show, I eavesdropped on people around me and I didn't hear any rapping about Jesus. I asked the waitress where the crowd was. She explained that the college students were just settling down to a new term and probably hadn't had much time to move out as yet. She also said that the Strip wasn't what it used to be and that the street action had moved over to Hollywood Boulevard.

I found that out.

3

Jesus, Come Quickly!

"How are you getting along with your parents?"

That was the question I heard again and again as I strolled along Hollywood Boulevard at night, eavesdropping on young Jesus People rapping with young prospects. I had to eavesdrop because the street-witnesses weren't talking to anybody who looked old enough to vote. It was easy to spot the Jesus People. They all carried Bibles.

Most of the girls wore long dresses. Most of the boys had long hair and/or beards; some of them wore headbands, and they were dressed in a modified variety of hippie garb. Actually, some of the youngsters they were approaching were dressed in similar clothes, so I deduced that it was the lack of a Bible that gave the prospects away.

I watched countless such approaches, on Hollywood Boulevard and on other Jesus People streets across the country, and often they were more like attacks. A prospect would appear, perhaps stepping off a bus or out of a car or through a door or just coming down the street, alone or with some friends. The Jesus People girls would approach a girl prospect in pairs; the boys approached a boy prospect in pairs. But the Jesus People streets were usually downtown streets, where the action was, and the prospects would come along as a group of two or three couples. The Jesus People would seem to materialize out of nowhere. Many times I saw them come running across the street to join an assault on a group of prospects. And then the questions: "Have you had your experience with the Lord yet? Have you given your life to Christ? Do you know Jesus died for your sins? How are you getting along with your parents?"

Since practically every teen-ager has had trouble of some kind with his parents at some time, there would be common grounds for rapping. The Jesus People would tell their story. So often it presented the same pattern. Trouble at home. Trouble at school. Drugs. Drinking. Sex. Running away. Destitution. Prostitution. Crashing. Getting busted. Back to the streets. Panhandling. More drugs and drinking and sex. Then suddenly Jesus. The Baptism. And peace and love and freedom from the Establishment.

The Jesus People know their Bible, and they believe in it completely. Studying the Bible is their major occupation after they have joined the Movement, most likely moving into a commune, and they learn to quote it freely, book, chapter and verse. Many times I heard this street argument: "God wrote the Bible. Men just put it down on paper for Him. Being God, God can't lie, and so everything in the Bible is true." And this: "Jesus said you must be born again if you want to be saved. Jesus said that unless you've had the Baptism in the Holy Spirit you're not a real Christian and you are heading for hell. The big thing to remember is that Jesus loves you. Until I found that out, I was a vegetable. But after I surrendered my life to Christ, I became a real human being and I got rid of all my hangups. This can happen to you."

This kind of witnessing was always done with tremendous fervor and intensity, always interspersed with Bible quotations, as though speaking upon the authority of the Bible overrode all debate. Often it did. Eavesdropping, I'd watch the faces of the prospects, usually in their upper teens, an age when all kids have hangups. With two well-trained Jesus People going at him simultaneously, the average prospect could do little but listen, and many of them listened attentively, their expressions of doubt gradually changing to curiosity, then interest. The longer that prospects were willing to rap, the more Jesus People gathered around them, until two or three prospects would be surrounded by as many as twenty Jesus People, all of them talking at once, all of them persistent and persuasive. In fact, their persuasiveness was so effective that I wondered what shape the country would be in if the Jesus People were advocating violence.

Some of the approaches ended quickly, sometimes rudely. I heard one boy say: "Yeah, man, but what has Jesus done for me lately?" And he walked off. At other times, a prospect, after rapping twenty minutes, a half hour, would, with what struck me as sincerity, accept some literature, and then depart with something like: "Okay, I'll be there tomorrow night," or "I can't make it 'til Friday, but I'll be there." At other times, a prospect or two would walk away with a few Jesus People, heading, as far as I could tell, to the group's headquarters, somewhere nearby. And at other times, there would be a vehicle parked nearby, a Volkswagen bus or even a school bus, and after a prospect seemed to come to a decision and start nodding his head, he would be led to the vehicle, helped into it, wait there, and when the car or bus was filled with prospects a Jesus Person would drive it away, presumably to headquarters.

I visited dozens of Jesus People headquarters, ranging from store fronts to rented houses to large farms. They all had one thing in common. Peace.

Up the road from Calvary Chapel, on the Costa Mesa side of the highway, stood an old farm house, set back perhaps twenty yards. Its front door faced a sideroad. As I approached the building, three young men were kneeling or sitting on the ground painting a short picket fence which enclosed a small yard of grass burned brown by the summer sun. The painters seemed in no hurry at their job. During the ten minutes I stood near them, they made hardly any progress at all. Two of them were bearded, the third being obviously too young. On the ground nearby was a cassette player, and I recognized the voice of Chuck Smith doing one of his taped sermons. While I was with them, the three young men did not speak to each other; but from time to time Chuck Smith evidently made a good point, for the young men would look at each other and nod. I was not sure whether they were aware of me. Finally I asked who was in charge.

One of them said: "Brother Marvin."

"Where can I find him?"

"Inside."

I wondered if I was violating some vow of silence. I headed for the house. On the porch steps sat a girl in a long dress, a Bible open on her lap. She was listening intently to Chuck Smith, and she did not look up as I passed. Inside, on the left, was a large room the length of the house. Folding chairs were along the wall, a few arm chairs; at the far end were two library-type tables. Two youths sat at one table, Bibles open before them; they were looking at each other and they may have been talking but I could not hear them. I proceeded toward the back of the house, passing two large bedrooms with several bunkbeds in them, two and three tiers high. At the back of the house I went down a few stairs into what was the kitchen and refectory. It was a large room, perhaps forty by sixty feet, and it appeared to be a new addition. Along the far wall were stoves and cooking utensils; on both sides of me were mess hall benches. Four or five girls were at the stoves, presumably preparing the evening meal. Near them, on the floor, perched on a blanket, were two babies not more than two years old, if that. They were just sitting there, looking about, not moving, not making a sound, and I was sure a lot of young parents would like to know how this was achieved.

When nobody paid any attention to me after a few minutes, I went to the girls and asked where I might find Brother Marvin. One of them nodded at a door in the corner. I headed for it, but the door opened and out came a young man who turned out to be Brother Marvin. He seemed deep in thought. He was wearing a full length robe and sandals. His black hair was down to his shoulders; his beard full. As we began to talk, he led me to the area of the benches but we did not sit down. He was soft-spoken; he looked away most of the time, and when he talked about himself he seemed to be fighting tears.

He was just eighteen. He was from a small city in Iowa where, while in high school, he started using LSD. He said: "I became a vegetable. I'd just about come off one trip and I'd take right off on another one. I couldn't study. I quit school. I couldn't eat. I was always sick. I never got any real rest. I knew I was killing myself but I couldn't stop it. Then I met a Christian girl, and she told me that the only way I could save myself was to come out here. So I took off."

"With your parents' permission?"

"My parents had given up on me."

Arriving in California, he made his way to Calvary Chapel where he got into conversations with other young people who were already in the Movement. He asked them what he could do to change his life. The answer was simple: give himself to Christ. "There wasn't anything else for me to do," Marvin told me, "so I went ahead with it. I was very desperate. I really prayed that Jesus would take over my life."

"And it worked?"
"Yes."
"Did you go through a sixty-second withdrawal?"
"Acid isn't like that. I just lost my need for it."
"Did you get the Baptism?"
"Yes."
"Right away?"
"Yes."
"Do you speak in tongues?"
"Yes. But it's the rule here to use tongues only for private devotions."
I asked: "Brother Marvin, is there a rule of silence in this house?"
"No," he said. "We believe that work is prayer and noise is childish. Our minds are always on the Lord." Eighteen years old.
Marvin told me that the house was one of a dozen similar communes in the immediate area, all of them affiliated with Calvary Chapel but self-supported. Also affiliated with the chapel was a farm in Oregon where leadership training was given those chosen to go out across the country to form new communes. Brother Marvin had made his commitment to the Lord about a year before I met him, which would make it September or October, 1970. He went through something like a basic training at a local commune and then was assigned to leadership studies in Oregon. From there he went to Reno, Nevada, to head a small commune there, and then he was brought back to Costa Mesa as head of the house, supervising the money and household assignments. I asked him where the money came from.
"Some of it is donations from people who know we are here," he said, "some of it is money our families send us, and some of it the boys earn by doing odd jobs around town. Wherever it comes from, it all goes into the common treasury to support the house."
"What shape are your finances usually in?"
"The Lord provides us with just enough."
"Does anybody have a full-time job?"
"You mean a weekly-payroll job? No. We don't have

the time. We have two periods a day of Bible study, private devotions, group devotions, prayer meetings at Calvary, and our street-witnessing. You can't hold a regular job, even part-time, with a schedule like that. We must always be ready to serve the Lord first."

Assigning household chores was simple enough. The girls did the woman's work; the boys did the man's. Whenever there was a shortage of girls for the kitchen or light housework, the boys pitched in. The boys did the heavy maintenance of the house and grounds. The welcome mat was out day and night to hippies and gypsies who needed a place to crash, and they could stay as long as they wanted. However, if they stayed more than a couple of days they were expected to contribute somehow to the support of the house, if only by doing chores. But Brother Marvin told me that the hippies and gypsies who weren't ready yet for the Lord usually didn't hang around long.

A pickup truck pulled up and several boys jumped off the back. From behind the wheel came, I learned, Brother Bob, in charge of all the local Calvary communes. He was older, though still not twenty-five. He was blonde, moderately bearded, tall and lean, in jeans, confident, outgoing, easier for talk. He showed me around the place, pointing out that the single boys bunked on the first floor, the single girls on the second floor with the marrieds. Crashers were similarly separated, with the overflow of boys being assigned to the attic.

Brother Bob was a native of the Los Angeles area. All his life, he had been a victim of wanderlust and, starting in his teens, spent his summers hitchhiking around the country. "I didn't know it," he told me, "but I was searching for God." About three years before I met him, Brother Bob was in North Carolina, bumming around, when he felt a great urge to go to Canada, to Vancouver, British Columbia, specifically. He hitchhiked in a northwest direction, reaching the Canadian border in the state of Washington, but the Canadian customs officers refused to let him enter the country because he only had fifteen dollars on him.

"There was only one thing I could think of to do," he

recalled as we strolled out to the front yard. "I prayed. I told God that if there was anything in Canada He wanted me to do I would do it, but He would have to get me in. The next time I tried it, I got in without any trouble at all."

In Vancouver, he was wandering through the downtown area one night when he came upon some Jesus People while they were witnessing. At first, he stood aside, listening, but then he found himself being drawn into the discussion. He told me: "These two girls kept rapping with me about the Holy Spirit. I knew about God, of course, but I didn't know about the Holy Spirit. I'd never read the Bible. These two girls told me how they'd been baptized in the Spirit and it knocked them off drugs and got their heads straight and put the joys of the Lord into their lives. Well, I didn't think I had any special problems. I'd fooled around with drugs and sex a bit, but nothing heavy, so I wasn't concerned about that. But I had never seen such happy people—that's what got me. Everybody seemed so happy. So they said they were going to their place for a prayer meeting and they invited people to come along. I went. There was a lot of singing and praying and speaking in tongues, and I felt good. Then these two girls asked me if I wanted the Baptism, and I said yes. They had me kneel down, they put their hands on my head, they started praying in tongues, and they prayed me into the Baptism. Wow. It felt great."

Brother Bob remained in Vancouver for a few weeks, and then he felt that the Holy Spirit wanted him to return to Los Angeles. Once home, he heard about Calvary Chapel and went out there. Just the sight of the chapel was enough to convince him that this was where the Holy Spirit was guiding him. He joined one of its communes. Some months later, he was sent to Oregon for leadership training. After being head of one of the Calvary communes for several months, he was appointed supervisor of all of them in the area.

I asked: "Is this what you are going to do for the rest of your life?"

He said: "I'll do whatever the Lord tells me to do with my life." He looked up at the building, up at its steeply slanted roof, and an expression of listening came over his face. Then he softly whispered: "Thank you, Lord." I watched him, waiting. He looked at me and said: "I've been wanting to get more space for this building. I've been thinking of building on a couple of rooms. The Lord just told me to get permission from the owner to raise the roof about fifteen feet and then we'll have room for another thirty people in the space we're losing to the slanting ceiling."

I asked: "Suppose the landlord doesn't give his permission?"

He was almost annoyed. "The Lord doesn't tell me to do things he knows won't work out." Again that faith.

I had left my briefcase in the kitchen and went for it. As I descended the stairs, I saw a young girl struggling across the room with a metal barrel filled with heads of lettuce. Before I could reach her to help, she had reached her destination—a wooden table—and she began shredding the lettuce, presumably for salad. I said hello to her and asked her name. Like so many Jesus People, she answered only with her first.

"Ann."

"Where are you from, Ann?"

"New York."

"New York City?"

"Yes."

"Where?"

"Manhattan."

"I live in Manhattan. Where?"

New Yorkers answer this question in terms of the nearest intersection. "West End and Seventy-fourth."

"We're neighbors. I'm on the Drive." No reaction. I asked: "How long have you been out here?"

"A year."

"What brought you out?"

"I got tired of the New York drug scene."

"What happened when you got here?"

"I went on the California drug scene."

"For how long?"

"Two months."

"What took you off?"

"A friend of mine became a Christian, and she talked me into it. That cured me."

"How long have you been in this place?"

"Ten months."

"You're happy?"

"Yes."

"Do your parents know where you are?"

"Yes."

"Do you keep in touch with them?"

"I write them once a month. It's the rule."

"How do they feel about all this?"

"They accept it."

"Well, Ann, now that you're off drugs and you're leading a Christian life, when do you think you'll go home?"

"I *am* home."

Before leaving New York on my trip, I studied the thick files on the Jesus Movement compiled by the *Guideposts* staff. The editors were interested in the Movement primarily because they felt it was a significant religious happening that deserved attention. Moreover, one of the editors—John Sherrill—had, through his books, unintentionally become an implementor of the Movement. Also, the mail from the readers indicated a growing interest in the gifts of the Holy Spirit, who had hardly been mentioned in the magazine in twenty years. Several times in the research I came upon the names of Tony and Susan Alamo, working in the Los Angeles area, and I made a mental note to contact them. But when I got to California and asked people about the Alamos, nobody knew where they were located. They were not in the telephone directory. Then a friend knew a friend who knew somebody who had once attended an Alamo prayer service, and I was given a lead to a certain block in North Hollywood. Nobody was home in the whole block, and the only building that looked as though it might have been a gathering place was abandoned. The bulletin board in front of it was bare. After two weeks of this, I had to leave for San Francisco. On my last morning, I was walking back to my hotel after an interview when, on Hollywood Boulevard, a teen-ager thrust into my hand a piece of paper, two by four inches. Over the past two weeks, I had been given dozens of bits of paper, usually containing a Bible quotation and warning me to repent of my sins. I glanced at this piece, decided it was the same, and had there been a waste basket nearby I would have thrown it away. Instead, I put it into my pocket. In my room, I changed, preparing for my trip north. On emptying my pockets, I saw the piece of paper and decided to take another look at it before throwing it away. This:

REPENT OF YOUR SINS
JESUS IS COMING SOON
Services Every Evening 8 P.M.
Sunday 3 P.M. and 8 P.M.
Tony and Susan Alamo
Christian Foundation
13136 Sierra Highway
Saugus, California
(805) 252-9842
Free Ride at Hollywood Blvd.
and Highland Ave.:
Mon. through Sat. at 6 P.M.
Sundays at 1:30 & 6:15 P.M.

So there they were. And I had almost thrown the piece of paper away. I called the number and was told that the Alamos had not arrived as yet, but I was given a Hollywood number where I could probably reach them. I called there. Tony Alamo answered, sounding as though I had awakened him. I identified myself, explained what I was doing, and then I told him how I had been looking for him and his wife for two weeks, had given up, and would have been on my way to San Francisco in an hour had I not decided to take a second look at a piece of paper that a boy had handed me on the street ten minutes before.

Tony Alamo said: "That's guidance for you."

"Right," I said, surprised to find myself already in tune with a people I was still trying to understand. We agreed to meet at Saugus in the afternoon.

The Tony and Susan Alamo Christian Foundation was the only Jesus People headquarters where I saw ash trays. I pointed this out to Susan, and she said: "Why not? I've never seen in the Bible, 'Thou shalt not smoke.'" Susan Alamo, fortyish, was the only woman I met on the Protestant side of the Jesus Movement who wore her hair up, used make-up lightly, and had jewelry. She was close to glamorous. She was also extremely witty, almost bitingly so as she told me about the trials and tribulation she and Tony had gone through during the five years they had been working in the Jesus Movement. The Alamos claimed, in fact, that they started the Movement, in that they were the first to go out into the streets and to help young dope addicts on the Strip and along Hollywood Boulevard.

The Alamos were Jews. Christian Jews. Tony's real name was Bernard Hoffman. He told me that he took the Italian name when, years ago, he started singing in nightclubs, believing that appearing to be Italian would be an advantage in view of the fact that most of the nightclubs were owned by Italians. Susan had become a Christian when she was a young girl. At the time, she had a skin disease. One evening she attended with a Christian girlfriend a service at a Pentecostal Church, and when she found herself responding to the altar call, the disease cleared up. Later she received the Baptism in the Holy Spirit and the gift of tongues. She brought her entire family to Christianity. She also became an ordained minister and was a popular preacher in Pentecostal churches in the Southwest.

Tony and Susan had known each other socially. Susan told me: "I couldn't stand him. Every time I saw him, he was surrounded by a bevy of beauties. I knew he was living in sin. I tried to talk to him a few times about the Lord, but I was wasting my breath."

From nightclubs, Tony went into the management of other performers and then into the recording business. He had a beautiful home at Malibu, and he was rich. One evening in 1965, Susan was having dinner alone in a restaurant when she saw Tony come in. The first thing she noticed about him was that he was alone, which was rare for him. The second thing she noticed was that he was obviously upset about something. He wasn't acting like himself at all. He glanced about, looking for the headwaiter, and then he saw Susan. He came quickly across the room and sat down at her table without being asked. He didn't even say hello. He seemed to be struggling for words.

Susan glanced at him, impatient and annoyed, and she wondered whether he had a hangover or was just working up to one. She said: "Tony, don't you know that Jesus Christ is coming soon?"

He looked at her as though she had slapped him. "Did he tell *you* that, *too?*" he exclaimed, and a great weight fell off him.

Susan dropped her fork. "What are you talking about?"

"The other night," he said, "at home, I woke up from a deep sleep in the middle of the night, and I got the feeling that somebody else was in the room. My first thought was robbers. I sat up. I looked around. And then I saw him. I saw Jesus Christ. I swear to you, Susan, it was Jesus Christ. We just looked at each other for about thirty seconds, and then he said: 'Tony, I am coming soon.' And then he disappeared. I've been a wreck ever since. I know I was awake and I know I was sober and I know this happened, but I've been afraid to tell people about it because I'm sure they'd think I'm crazy. Then I saw you just now. Susan, you are the only person who can explain this to me. You are the only person who could believe me." A waiter came up and asked Tony what he wanted to drink. Tony waved the man away.

Susan said: "I believe you, Tony. Only a personal appearance by Jesus Christ himself could make you turn down a drink."

They sat there for hours, Tony with a thousand questions about Jesus Christ and the Bible, Susan with the answers. Susan didn't get to finish her food; Tony didn't order any. The restaurant emptied out. Busboys stripped the tables and piled chairs on them. The headwaiter finally had to come over and ask Tony and Susan to leave. They went to Susan's apartment, where she prayed Tony into the Baptism. Tony quit his job, dropped his other clients, and then undertook the studies which qualified him for ordination. He and Susan became a team of popular preachers on the Pentecostal circuit. Two years later, they were married.

One night as they were heading home their route took them along Sunset Strip, already a haven for hippies, runaways, pushers, addicts. The Alamos had heard about this trend, but they hadn't given it much thought—it just wasn't part of their lives. And now they were seeing it all with their own eyes.

Susan said: "Tony, this is awful. These kids are lost. We've got exactly what they're all looking for, but we've been expecting them to come to us and ask for it. Park the car, Tony."

Tony parked the car; the two of them got out, and they started to stop the strolling youngsters and talk to them about the Lord. This was in 1966, and the Alamos claimed it was the beginning of street-evangelizing on the Strip. In an hour, they had a half dozen kids standing by, waiting to hear more, but they had no place to take them. Tony said: "Let's take them home, Su. Maybe you could cook something up for them. They look like they could use something to eat."

So they took the kids home, let them wash up, fed them, and then talked some more to them about Christ. That night, all the kids committed their lives to Jesus. When it got late, Tony asked if he could give the kids a lift to wherever they intended to spend the night. They all said they didn't have a place and would probably sleep out on the beach. Susan wouldn't hear of this, and so make-shift sleeping arrangements were set up all over the house. And this, too, was a beginning.

Because they were popular, the Alamos' preaching schedule was booked months in advance. But now something was happening to them. On nights when it was possible, they went to the Strip after a service; on nights they were free, they were there early. And there was always a gang of kids at their house at Malibu. Gradually Tony and Susan Alamo became aware that their ministry was changing; and they began to feel that when they were away from the Strip, away from the kids, they were not doing what the Lord really wanted of them. And there was something else. In their church sermons, the Alamos started referring more and more to the kids, to their needs, to their problems at home and in life that had put them on the streets. As time went on, the Alamos sensed that the people in the churches didn't care much about the kids and weren't much interested in them. Month by month, the Alamos decreased their church appearances and eventually eliminated them, becoming, in time, about as anti-church as anyone I met in the Jesus Movement.

There was the matter of money. As preachers, the Alamos had been able to earn a living, and they were able to continue living in Tony's house at the beach, which was already paid for. But as they withdrew from church work, they also withdrew from their source of income. They soon found themselves living on their savings and investments, and this might have lasted longer if they had only themselves to support. They were supporting, in fact, most of the kids they took home and brought to the Lord, and their money was disappearing fast.

The day came when they had to face facts, and they faced them quite unrealistically. They decided that their house was too small and also too far from the Strip. So they sold the house and, a couple of blocks off the Strip, rented a mansion that had a huge living room. Knowing that kids liked music, that it was music that drew them into the coffeehouses where the dope peddling was wide open, the Alamos purchased instruments for the kids they had who could play them. In effect, they turned the living room into a coffeehouse. They acquired an audience by passing out fliers during the street-witnessing, offering the kids rock music, free coffee and even a free ride to the mansion. All promises were kept, except that the rock music was rock hymns. Tony found himself back in show business, singing while he led the singing. Some of the Alamos' new Christians would then witness, and then either Tony or Susan would preach. At the finish, there would be an altar call—a stage call, more correctly. The Alamos wondered at first if some of the audience might feel they had been conned into going to a coffeehouse that was virtually a church. Some of them did, and they walked out as soon as they realized what was going on. But the rest of them thought that singing the old songs to rock was a lot of fun, they were impressed by the witnessing, and they were carried away by the fiery and forceful sermons, the likes of which most of them had not heard since they were kids back home and their parents took them to revivals. The responses to the altar call were always good. If any of the youngsters, on committing their lives to Christ, experienced the Baptism in the Holy Spirit at the same time, the Alamos invited them to move in so that they could start getting the Bible training that could make them steadfast in their new faith. The kids kept moving in. And the money kept moving out.

Because of the turn which the Alamos' lives had taken, they began to lose some of their friends, particularly their church-affiliated friends, and in the course of the severance Susan would tell them: "We're doing your work, you know. You should be taking these kids into your churches, you should be bringing them to the Lord, you should be helping them settle down and build new lives. Because you're not, don't be surprised when you find your churches empty."

But new friends appeared. A baker sent over his unsold bread at the end of the day. A grocer gave his unsold perishable vegetables. He once sent over a hundred-pound sack of beans, and everybody ate mostly beans for a few days. Friends also appeared in the form of parents of some of the youngsters. On moving into the mansion, the first thing a boy or girl had to do was clear up their relationship with their parents, whether this meant writing a letter, making a phone call or going home for a few days. Parents visited the house to find out what had changed their children so dramatically, they were satisfied with what they saw, and many of them made donations, some on a steady basis. Another matter that had to be resolved right away was a boy's draft status. If he hadn't registered, if he had lost or destroyed his draft card or if he was eluding induction, he had to straighten himself out with the draft board before he'd be allowed to remain in the group. Similarly, anybody who was wanted by the law had to clear up that matter before being allowed to remain. One boy, for example, who had escaped from an Eastern reformatory where he had been sent for stealing cars, went back to serve out his time once he understood how the Alamos felt about restitution. As Susan put it: "Becoming a Christian gives you a new life, but it doesn't release you from responsibility for your old life."

The activities at the mansion continued for three months. From the start, the neighbors complained about the noise, and so the living room was sound-proofed. But the neighbors went on and on with their complaints about the kind of people who were wandering around the neighborhood. Out of this came police harassment. As with Arthur Blessitt's *His Place,* the police walked into the house whenever they felt like it, without search warrants, and they frisked people. In view of the face that every night there were new people present for the first time, it wasn't surprising that some of them had drugs on them. Tony was arrested twice, Susan once, but they were both acquitted. One night all hundred and fifty people in the place were taken away in police vans. Finally enough pressure was put on the owner for him to tell the Alamos that he had sold the building to his son-in-law, who wanted to occupy it, and they would have to move.

As they looked around for a new place, the Alamos tried to proceed with their work by holding small meetings in their apartment. Always they had the worry of kids who had no place to sleep. Countless times Tony said: "Then you can stay here. You may have to sleep in a closet, but we'll find room for you somehow."

Eventually they found enough room for everybody. In Beverly Hills, they located a building that had been zoned as a church, and it was a block off the Strip. There were rooms that could be used for Bible studies, rooms that could be used for sleeping quarters, there were cooking facilities and a big auditorium. The Alamos decided they no longer needed the front of a coffeehouse: they were in the Lord's business, and anybody who entered the place would know that. Also, they were becoming well-known in what the country was gradually recognizing as an important religious movement. Moreover, they were getting publicity, usually as a result of the raids and arrests at the mansion, and though it was bad publicity it nevertheless brought in the curious.

The money problems persisted. At one point, they were a hundred and fifty dollars short of their rent at the new building, and they didn't want to risk their already shaky position with the owner by being late. As they were wondering how they could raise the money, they got an invitation from the Full Gospel Businessmen's Association, of Long Beach, to tell the story of the work at an Association luncheon.

Tony asked: "How do they expect us to tell our story in the twenty minutes they'll probably allot us?"

Susan said: "Let's not tell *our* story. Let's have the kids tell *theirs.*"

"Have the kids witness?" Tony asked.

"Why not? The kids are what this is all about."

"Won't that seem a little strange? After all," Tony said, "we were the ones who were invited."

"Yes, we were invited, and we'll go," said Susan, "and we'll just take along a few friends."

"How many?"

"A bus load."

They managed to get about a hundred kids on the bus. At Long Beach, the kids had a picnic lunch outdoors while the Alamos lunched with the people at the gathering. When the time came for the talk, the kids were brought in and lined up behind the head table. The sight of them, all hippie types, surprised the people to the point that there was scarcely a sound in the room during their entrance.

Then Susan Alamo stepped to the microphone and said: "Ladies and gentlemen, if you, as Christians, consider yourselves to be brothers and sisters, I want you to meet some more of your brothers and sisters in Christ Jesus. As you listen to them, ask yourselves how you could ever turn them away. Tony and I could not."

One by one, the kids stepped to the microphone and told their stories of what their lives had been like before their commitments to Christ and what their lives were like now. Even before half the youngsters had spoken, someone in the audience got the message and began to pass a hat. When the witnessing was over, the collection was given to the Alamos. It was exactly one hundred and fifty dollars.

The real problem the Alamos were having was an old one—their neighbors. Next door was a swanky apartment house occupied by movie stars and socialites, and these people did not want hordes of hippies cluttering up their block. The police harassment began again, mostly on charges of drugs on the premises. On one occasion, the police produced as evidence a hypodermic needle that they found in front of the building. The Alamos were unable to convince the police that addicts were not that careless with their equipment and that the needle had probably been thrown away by someone who, on committing himself to Christ in the church decided he didn't need it anymore. But this sort of thing kept happening until, by a court order, the Alamos had to close down.

They realized they would have to get out of the city. It was the only way they could survive. Since they were apparently going to have trouble with neighbors and the police no matter where they tried to settle in the Los Angeles area, the best thing was to find a place where they could be by themselves, away from neighbors and, hopefully, the police. Susan knew about a piece of property at Saugus, thirty miles out of town. It was owned by a church and, years ago, she had gone there a few times on church picnics. Since then, the church had leased the property to some people who had built a nightclub there, but the club had gone out of business. Susan and Tony drove up to inspect the property, about eight acres. Vandals had been at the main building; it was a mess, but it could be repaired and most of the kitchen equipment could be salvaged. Checking, the Alamos learned that the church was willing to sell.

The Lord provided the money to buy. Now, you can say that to a Jesus Person and he will not blink an eyelash. Practically all of the leaders of the Movement whom I interviewed told me that, in one way or another, the Lord provided the means for him to begin and to survive. Sometimes the means arrived in one fell swoop, sometimes it dribbled in at the right moment, at other times a banker found himself being unexpectedly lenient on terms for a loan, and at other times the owner of a piece of property or a building or a bus or just a barrel of apples suddenly couldn't wait to turn over whatever it was to the Jesus People. Of all the groups I met, only two subsequently sent me fund-raising letters. The rest told me that they didn't ask people for money—they asked the Lord. And the Lord provided.

So the Lord provided the Alamos with the means to acquire the land and buildings. One day, they loaded their kids on buses and, full of joy and song, they all went to their new home. As they got off the bus, they were handed tools, and they started putting their new home into shape. Since then, the Lord has provided the means for the Alamos to acquire about four hundred acres along the Sierra Highway, including a farm that will eventually produce most of the foodstuffs necessary to support the commune.

Susan Alamo told me: "This isn't a commune in the usual sense. We separate the sexes. The unmarried boys have quarters here at the main building. The unmarried girls and the married couples have their own area about five miles down the road." I asked Susan if she thought that the unmarrieds were participating in sex of any kind. With unique honesty, she said: "I would have to assume that they do, but I'm sure they're not doing as much of it as they did before they came here." I asked her what the commune's population was, and she said: "I won't tell you because we have too much, but I will tell you that we serve fifteen hundred meals a day."

The main building still resembled a nightclub. There were booths along the length of it; in three or four of them, boys were at their Bible studies. The spacious dance floor was now the chapel, folding chairs piled up in the back. The Alamos told me that their nightly congregation averaged around four hundred, but they have had crowds of seven hundred packed in the place. Beyond was the twenty-four-hour-a-day prayer room. The door to it was locked with a simple hook-and-eye device. We went inside and Tony closed the door behind us. Except for a small amber ceiling light in one corner, the room was in darkness. As my eyes became adjusted to the room, I saw a few pieces of furniture scattered about a room of perhaps forty-by-forty feet. Five or six boys were in the room. One was stretched out on a sofa and might have been asleep. The others were standing, facing the light, supporting themselves on furniture, and they were all praying in tongues at the tops of their voices. One boy was shaking severely. The air was moist and foul, and as we stood there perhaps four or five minutes an uneasiness came over me and I felt a bit dizzy. I was relieved when Tony opened the door and we went out. Susan told me that the girls had a similar room where praying in tongues went on around the clock.

I asked: "Do all your kids have the Baptism?"

Susan said: "We don't take them unless they do."

I said: "Supposing a kid came here, an addict, say, in pretty bad shape, and he realized you could help him and he wanted to stay but he hadn't received the Baptism yet —what would you do?"

"It's doesn't work that way," Susan said. "The kid doesn't realize that *we* can help him: he realizes that *Jesus* can help him. If he really wants to change his life, he commits himself to Jesus, and he gets the Baptism. That makes him one of us, and he can stay as long as he likes."

"I've been told," I said, "that not everybody who receives the Baptism speaks in tongues right away."

"They do here," she said, matter-of-factly.

We looked around. The youngsters were not as glum as those I had met in the small commune in Costa Mesa. There was a great deal of activity here. The Bible studies in the booths were more animated. There was steady traffic to a coffee urn; some of the kids were smoking. I could tell the newcomers by the wonderment on their faces as an advanced Bible student explained certain points. In the several rooms that comprised the kitchen some thirty cooks were at work, mostly boys. In one room, a phonograph was playing a recorded sermon but I did not recognize the preacher. The boys were more casual with each other than those at Costa Mesa. I actually saw some smiles. Everybody brightened at the sight of Tony and Susan Alamo. From time to time, someone would take Susan or Tony aside to talk, and it seemed to me that the Alamos' relationships with the kids were personal, confident and loving.

Susan told me: "Tony and I really have little to do with running this place. The kids run it. They choose their own supervisors, and the supervisors make the job assignments. Everybody here works and earns enough to keep himself in personal things. Nobody is allowed to be on welfare. The only public assistance that is acceptable is Medical for a girl who is pregnant when she gets here or a married girl who gets pregnant. Otherwise, we pay our own way. It's up to the kids to see to it. They handle the money as it comes in and they do the buying. I don't even know how much we have in the bank, but I can find out if you want to know."

A newcomer is required to stay on the grounds for his first six months, studying the Bible, doing his chores and spending his hour a day in the prayer room. After that, he spends four hours a day street-witnessing in the surrounding town and in the city. At this point, he is allowed to take a job, if he can find one, on the surrounding farms and in the towns, and he continues to live at the commune. He is not required to tithe, but all those who were employed voluntarily gave ten percent of their salary to the commune.

We went to the area where the single girls and the married couples lived. Parked here were the buses used for bringing people in from the surrounding towns and the city. Several boys and young men were working on them, cleaning them, tuning engines, and one was being painted. A few small children were wandering about, watching. The main building had a day room, large and attractive. Some girls were at their Bible studies. Beyond was the nursery, with a few babies and tots in it, and two girls were in attendance. The Alamos told me that the building was going to be enlarged to provide more room for study and food preparation. At the time, food was being brought down from the headquarters in containers. Work on the expansion had already started.

I inspected the small structures where the married couples lived. The buildings had once been rabbit hutches, about seven-by-ten feet, but they had been cleaned up, painted and decorated. A few of them had little gardens. The interiors were compact but pleasant, and a few of them had cribs.

Chores for the girls were mostly the laundry and sewing, some cooking, and taking care of the children. The girls had their own around-the-clock prayer room, but I did not see it. Qualified girls also did street-witnessing. I asked one girl how long she had been there, and she said: "Five months."

"Then you'll soon be street-witnessing, won't you?"

"Yes. I'm looking forward to it."

"What do you think is the most important thing you'll have to say to people?"

"Jesus is coming."

The word is Maranatha. It appears only once in the Bible, and there is some difference of opinion as to what it means. The concordance puts it as Maran-atha, and says: "An Aramaic or Syrian expression used by St. Paul at the conclusion of his First Epistle to the Corinthians, 1 Cor 16:22, meaning our Lord cometh." My King James includes the word in the single sentence of the verse, thusly: "If any man love not the Lord Jesus Christ, let him be Anathema Maranatha." Both the Catholic Confraternity and Douay editions put the word in a sentence by itself at the end of the verse, and both have this footnote: "The Aramaic *Maran atha* means, 'The Lord comes.' By another division of the letters, *Marana tha,* one gets, 'Our Lord, come.' " The New English Bible puts it: *"Marana tha*—Come O Lord!" The Revised Catholic Standard version has: "Our Lord, come!" and the footnote: "Greek *Maranatha."* Duane Pederson told me that it was Greek and, to the Jesus People, meant: "Lord, come quickly!"

And this is the core of the Jesus People Movement—

the Second Coming of Jesus Christ. Soon. In our time. This was why Duane Pederson kept telling me to read the newspapers and read the Bible. The Jesus People believe that the Bible prophecies pertaining to the Second Coming are now being fulfilled and are in the headlines of our daily papers.

The Jesus People maintain that we are in the End Times. This expression is derived from Daniel 11:40, which begins: "At the time of the end," the end being the threshold of the return of Christ. Christians have always believed that Jesus would return. The early Christians, including Paul himself, thought Jesus would return in their own time. During Christ's ministry, the Apostles asked him when he was going to come back, and he told them not to bother their heads about it, that this was something that only the Father knew. Even so, some Bible research, as done by Hal Lindsey, whom I did not meet, and Ray C. Stedman, whom I did, has resulted in some effective, if circumstantial, evidence that the time is well nigh.

According to men like Lindsey and Stedman, who worked separately, incidentally, the early Jewish exegetists did not realize that the Messiah was going to come twice, first, to save the world and second, to claim it. So there appeared to be some contradictions among the early prophets. Some of them said the Messiah would come as a babe, born in a manger; others said he would come as a great king, with a great army, and rescue the Jews from their enemies. At the time Jesus was born in a manger, the Jewish lands were occupied by the Romans, and the Jews very much needed a great king with a great army. It was for this reason that the Jewish leaders couldn't believe that, at a time of such crisis, the Messiah would be born in a barn, grow up in the home of a carpenter, and practice this trade himself before coming out of nowhere and beginning his ministry at the age of thirty. They therefore rejected him, as was predicted, they had him crucified, as was predicted, and a few years later the Temple was destroyed and the Jews were dispersed, as was predicted.

Hundreds—thousands—of years before Jesus was born, it was prophesied by Moses and Ezekiel and Daniel and

Zachariah that before the Second Coming, although they didn't call it that) the Jews would re-establish themselves in their own nation. Over the centuries since the Crucifixion, very few historians, even Bible scholars, really believed that this would ever come about. The Jews were too scattered, they had no organization, and they never, despite anti-Semitic propaganda, gained enough power as a people in another country to get that country to back them in a war to regain their homeland back. It seemed impossible. And yet it happened. In 1948, with the help of Zionists around the world, the Jews of the world fought the war that resulted in the partitioning of Palestine and the creation of the State of Israel.

According to the prophets, the generation born at the time the Jews got their country back would be the generation that would witness the return of Jesus. But now there was no dispute about that. The Bible said that, before the Messiah came, the Jews would not only regain their country but they would hold Jerusalem and they would pray at the Temple. In 1948, the Jews held only a part of Jerusalem, and they wouldn't get anywhere near the Temple. For centuries the Temple had been the Mosque of Omar, a sacred place for Muslims, and all that remained of the structure which stood there in 70 A.D. was the wailing wall, sacred to the Jews. Then, in 1967, in a six day war, the Jews not only took over all of Jerusalem, they took over other land that had once been theirs, plus quite a bit that wasn't. The dispute dividing the experts was this: Was the last generation born in 1948 or 1967? But there was still another matter. The Bible said that the Temple would be rebuilt before the Messiah arrived. Although, in 1967, the Jews could pray at the wailing wall for the first time in nineteen hundred years, the building itself was still the Mosque of Omar. The Israelis had announced early that high on their list of priorities for Jerusalem was the rebuilding of the Temple, but they must have realized it would be unwise to rush into this. In 1972, the Jews still had only the wall. The Arab-Israeli War really was not over, and the support of the Israeli position really was not so universal that they could risk the audacity of tearing down a shrine, even a Muslim shrine, without world repercussions. So the experts had another question: Would the generation born at the time of the rebuilding of the Temple be the last generation to reach maturity before the Second Coming? Nobody could be sure. Even Jesus did not seem to know. All he said was that it would be better for the rest of us not to be around when he came back.

Meanwhile, other pieces of the puzzle began to fall into place. The Bible said that, before the Second Coming, ten nations of Europe would become federated into a single country. The European Common Market, organized in 1958, had, in 1972, six members—Belgium, France, Italy, Luxembourg, the Netherlands and West Germany, and the membership of Great Britain had just been approved. Seven. Applying for membership were Denmark, Norway and Ireland. Ten. The Bible said that this new, in effect, United States of Europe will become the richest and strongest nation in the world. A leader will appear, a Roman, and he will become the most powerful man on the earth. He will seem to be a good man, in that he will solve many problems of the world, but he will solve them not through wisdom and goodness but by his own strength. In Jerusalem, a religious leader will claim that the European dictator is the returned Christ, and many people will believe this. The Christian Church of today will be transformed beyond recognition. The European will demand—and receive—obeisance, reverence and adoration from most people. Christians who choose to live by their Bible faith will be persecuted as never before, and eventually they will be eliminated.

While this is going on, the Arab nations will unite to form a mighty military force, and, in alliance with Russia, will attack Israel. But the Russians will move faster, overrunning Israel, then proceeding onward and outward to overrun the Arab world and all of Africa. The European ruler, by now considered to be God by his people, will go to war against the Russians, attacking mainly at Israel. By then the United States will be a third-rate power and will go along with Europe. The Orient will also side with Europe, attacking from the east. It is while this war is going on, with the whole world involved, if only in the suffering, that Jesus Christ will return, accompanied by a vast army of saints. The saints will be the good Christians who have lived and died up to this time. Then begins the last war, the Armageddon, the war between good and evil, and goodness will triumph. Upon the victory, Jesus Christ will give the faith to one hundred forty-four thousand of the surviving Jews, twelve thousand from each of the twelve tribes, and these people will go out and do what they were told to do once before—evangelize the world, what is left of the world. They will succeed this time. There will be a thousand years of peace, with Jesus Christ as the ruler of the world. Then Judgment Day, and the end of it all.

The Jesus People believe all this wholeheartedly. And they can't wait for it to happen. They can quote you chapter-and-verse to prove that it is going to happen. They back themselves up by quoting chapter-and-verse of other prophecies that were fulfilled. The only question is: When?

A generation is usually put at forty years. If, then, the last generation to be born before the Second Coming was born upon the birth of Israel in 1948, Jesus should return around 1988. Because of the events which are to precede his return, this would mean that the man who is to become the God of Europe is already alive and perhaps already on the political scene. The Bible said he would be a Roman, but it should be remembered that at one time most of Europe was part of the Holy Roman Empire, and so he could come from any country on the continent. Also alive is the false prophet who will acclaim this man to be Jesus Christ. If, however, the last generation was born after the 1967 war, there are a couple of little boys around somewhere who are destined to lead the world into its worst days. But if the generation is to be determined by the reconstruction of the Temple, then it's anybody's guess. Few of the Jesus People with whom I discussed this subject favored the Temple theory. Between a quarter and a third supported the 1967 prospect. The rest all held to 1948. Because of their present youth, many of the Jesus People I met should still be around when things begin to happen.

They can't wait. Not one of the Jesus People I met

viewed the future with any regret or fear. They believe that by their commitment to Christ, by their Baptism in the Holy Spirit and by the lives they are leading now, they are strengthening themselves spiritually for the battle against the missionaries of the Anti-Christ who will seek to destroy Christianity by destroying Christians. If they must die for Jesus Christ, very well: they point out to you that he once died for them. And if they die, then they will return with the army of saints and fight evil for Jesus. But the Jesus People also believe that some of them will survive the terror. It is, according to the Bible, to last only seven years. That's not a long time to spend in the new catacombs. Then, after the victory, there would be cells of Christians around the world, in the mountains, in forests, in deserts, on remote islands, ready to cooperate with the evangelizing Jews in building a new world of peace and brotherhood and love.

And Jesus would be here.
I heard it so often.
"Jesus is coming soon."
"Maranatha!"

4

And A Child Shall Lead Them...

The evening I telephoned the Los Angeles Teen Challenge Center, a girl named Dixie told me that the professional staff had left for the day but that two group therapy sessions were going to be held that evening and I could sit in on them if I wished. The center was one of sixty which Dave Wilkerson had opened across the country after the success of the book the Sherrills had written for him. By policy, most of the residents had been addicts who, for one reason or another, turned to religion for help. Unlike other Jesus People facilities, the Teen Challenge centers usually have had a staff of psychotherapists, social workers, ministers, career counselors and nurses. Also unlike other places of the same type, the residents need not have had the Baptism before acceptance, and they can stay on as long as they want without making any effort to receive it. However, most of them do experience it early in their stay.

I was surprised by the location of the Los Angeles center. Most of the centers were located in or near ghettos, following Wilkerson's first effort among the blacks and Puerto Ricans of Brooklyn. The Los Angeles center was on South Hobart, a quiet, tree-lined street, surrounded by homes that were definitely of upper-middle-class value. The center had two houses, one for girls and one for boys, and the girls' house was practically a mansion. Dixie told me it was the best house they'd had.

I visited with the girls first; their session had already begun when I got there, with Dixie as the moderator. It was very informal. Some of the girls were sitting on the floor, others had their legs thrown over the arm of a chair, and most of them had their shoes off. They ranged from their upper teens to their early twenties, and there were about twenty of them. They were all white. There didn't seem to be any special theme to the meeting, and it was more like a let's-clear-the-air session.

One girl said: "Lately Dora's been acting like she's too good for us. Every time Emma and I come around, she walks away. She didn't even finish her meal tonight because Emma and I sat down at her table."

"That's not true," said Dora, which wasn't her name. "I didn't finish my meal because I'm trying to lose some weight."

Emma said: "Bull. Then why did you walk out of the prayer room yesterday when Ellen and I walked in?"

"Because I was finished."

Emma said: "Bull."

Dora said: "All right, then. I don't like being around you two because you are always putting me down. You needle heads are all alike. Just because a person was only on pills, you think it's kid stuff and she's chicken."

Ellen, the accuser, asked: "When did we ever say that?"

"You're saying something like that all the time," Dora said. She turned to another girl. "Millie, what did Ellen say to you last week when you first got here, when she asked you what you were on and you said you popped junk?"

Millie nodded, agreeing with Dora. "She said: 'Okay. Hang around. Us hypes have to stick together.' But I just thought that she wanted to be friends."

Dixie broke in. "Right. We're all friends here. It doesn't make any difference what we were strung out on. We're sisters, sisters in the Lord. We're Christians, and we should treat each other like Christians. When we look at each other, we should see the Christ in each other, and we should all love each other equally. It was Christ who brought us here, and it's Christ who is going to solve our problems."

Someone said: "I wish I could believe that." I looked. She seemed a bit older than the others, small, thin, bony face, small dark eyes, her black hair cut short. Her expression was part challenge, part sadness.

Dixie said: "Well, Helen, Jesus won't be able to help you unless you believe it."

"I've tried," Helen said. "I've told Jesus out loud that I believed that he could help me, but he hasn't done anything. I've been in and out of this place a dozen times, but the same thing keeps happening."

Dixie said: "That's because you keep going back to your girlfriend."

"Look," said Helen, "my 'ole lady' was a junkie when I met her and she will be a junkie for the rest of her life. I've argued with her, I've prayed for her, I've begged her to come here and get her head straightened out. She just laughs and kisses me, and in three days I'm hooked again."

"You shouldn't go back to her," said Dixie.

"But I'm in love with her," Helen insisted. "She's all I've got in the world. If Jesus wants me to give her up, what's he going to give me in her place?"

"Keep believing," Dixie said. "Keep praying." She turned to another girl. "Ann, how are you doing? I've noticed you seem to be in a better mood these last few days."

Ann had long blond hair. She was pretty, and her plumpness seemed to be part of her prettiness. She was smiling. "I'm doing all right, I guess," she said. "I keep praying about it, of course. I know that I'm not just another dirty doper anymore. I know I'm clean. I know that Jesus loves me and that this is what makes me important as a human being. I know that Jesus is with me all the time; I know that he is part of me and I am part of him. I'm beginning to like myself a little. I'm beginning to like my sisters here."

Dixie said: "Yes. Praise the Lord. I've noticed, Ann. I can see what the Lord is doing for you."

"Thanks," Ann said, and then she looked across the room. "Dora, are you serious about losing some weight?"

"I've been thinking about it."

"Let's go on a diet together, Dora," Ann said. "It'll be fun. It'll give us something to talk about."

Dora said: "All right. That's a good idea. Ann, Dixie is right. I can really see the Lord in you these days."

"Thanks."

It went on like that.

The boys' house was much smaller. The dozen people in the living room made it crowded. No group therapy was going on. Visitors had evidently arrived unexpectedly—a woman in her thirties, her husband who seemed much younger and her son who was around twenty. They were Spanish. Mexicans, perhaps. From what I could gather from the conversation, the young man had been arrested for possession of narcotics and was out on bail. It came out during the conversation that the woman and her husband had received the Baptism, and they had brought the son here with the hope that he would go on the program to overcome his addiction. In the room were eight or nine of the boys living in the house, four of them black, one Oriental, the rest white, and they seemed to range in age from around fifteen, the Oriental, to twenty-two or three, one of the blacks. Asleep on the floor was a huge German shepherd dog.

The woman and her husband said next to nothing during the next hour. The boys were witnessing to the young Mexican, and one black said: "I kicked drugs eighteen times. I was living with this chick who kicked drugs twenty-four times. The best we could do was five days. Then we'd get hooked again. The day I gave my problems to Jesus Christ, I was cured." The Mexican was not disbelieving; he was just not sure.

Another black asked him: "Do you believe in the Bible?"

"How do you mean?"

"Do you believe that everything in the Bible is the truth?"

"I don't know. I never read the Bible. We never had one in the house. When I was a kid, I went to church, but that was just Mass." (I was tempted to tell him that without the Bible there would be no Mass, but my place now was to listen.)

The black went on: "Do you believe in God?"

"Oh, yeah, sure. I believe in God."

"Do you believe that Jesus Christ is His son?"

"I suppose, but I don't know how that's possible."

"Do you believe that God write the Bible?"

"He did?"

"Well, men wrote it, but God told them what to put down."

"Oh."

"Do you believe that God lies?"

"Lies? Tells lies?"

"Yes. Do you believe that God, being God, would lie to us?"

"Maybe if He had a reason."

"Hey, man, God is truth. God can't lie."

"All right."

"Do you believe that?"

"All right."

"All right, then. Then everything that God told men to

write down in the Bible has to be the truth because God can't lie."

"All right."

"There's your answer. Move in here, we'll teach you everything that's in the Bible, all you have to do is live by what God says, and you won't have any problems with drugs or anything else."

On my trip I heard variations of this rationale many times, and I wondered how anything so specious could be so effective.

But the Mexican said: "I dunno."

Sitting next to the Mexican on the studio couch was a young black, still in his teens, tall and lean. He asked the Mexican: "Do you believe in the Devil?"

"No," the Mexican said firmly. "That's one thing I don't believe in. If God made everything, why should He make devils?"

The black said: "God didn't make devils. They used to be angels but they disobeyed God and that's how they became devils."

The Mexican looked inquiringly across the room at his mother. Her eyes met his. He asked: "Is that how it happened?" She nodded and looked away. He said: "All right."

The young black said: "I saw the Devil last night. I even fought him." Everybody looked at him. Suddenly animated, he moved to the edge of the couch. He used his hands a lot as he spoke, in the air and on himself, and he told us this:

"Last night, I went to services at a church I'd rather not mention by name. I disapprove of its theology. But I feel I ought to listen to everybody's ideas, so I go there once in a while. There was an altar call, and I went forward. I was standing there, waiting for the blessing, when I felt this hand on my leg, playing with me, feeling me up, trying to turn me on." He stood up and demonstrated.

Then he sat down, and he said: "Well, you guys know why I'm here. I didn't come thirty-five hundred miles just to kick drugs. I don't have a drug problem. I have another problem, and letting a man fool around with me, even that much, is something I can't permit. I thought it was the man on my right, and I looked at him, but he had his hands folded at his chest, like he was praying, so I knew it couldn't be him. I looked behind me and there were two women, and I didn't expect that either one of them would do anything like that. I could still feel the hand on me, and I was getting into trouble. I looked down but I couldn't see anything. That's when I began to realize what must be going on. I looked at that man again. I stepped back and I looked at him real hard. That's when I saw the Devil. I discerned the Devil in this man. So I moved to him and I whispered: 'Excuse me, sir, but I've got to tell you something. You're possessed. You've got a devil in you.' He looked at me like I was crazy, and he said in his regular voice: 'What are you talking about?' I told him. I told him again, and I said: 'We'd better get that devil out of you before we *both* go to hell.' So he said: 'What is all this? So I said: 'Mister, the Holy Spirit has given me the gift of discerning spirits, and I discern one in you right now. I'm going to try to exorcise you and I don't know what's going to happen, so be ready for anything.'

"By then, the service had stopped and everybody was looking at us. I backed away from the man and I looked the Devil right in the eyes, and I said: 'Devil, what is your name? And the Devil said: 'Beelzebub.' So I knew I was right. And I said: 'Beelzebub, in the name of Jesus Christ I command you to leave that man's body and go back to hell.' But the Devil said: 'I won't.' I said: 'You have to. I demand it in Jesus' name.' Well, the man began to shake something awful. I knew it was the Devil, fighting to stay in there, so I said: 'All right, Beelzebub, if you want a fight, you're gonna get one. I'll fight you with the strength of Jesus Christ!' The man fell to the floor even before I got to him. I jumped on him and we started to fight—me and the Devil, I mean. The man was fighting me, but I knew it really wasn't him doing it; it was the Devil in him. Well, I don't know how long it went on. We were all over the floor. Some men who didn't know what was going on try to stop me, but I wouldn't let them and I put up a real battle. Finally the man sorta collapsed in a heap and I stopped. I looked at him and I couldn't see the Devil. I looked and I couldn't see the Devil anywhere in the church, so I knew he was gone. I got up and I apologized to the man if I hurt him, and I said: 'But I saved your soul, so you should thank God.' I knew that people were wondering what was going on, so I said: 'I cast a devil out of him.' And I left.

"When I got here, I went up to my room. Right away, I got the feeling that I wasn't alone. My roommate came in and I told him what happened, and I told him I felt the Devil was in the room and he'd better get out while he could. He left. I looked around, and there was the Devil in the corner. I knew I was going to have to fight him again. I also knew that he had something else on his mind besides the fight. I knew that if he overpowered me he would—well, I was ready to die rather than let that happen. So we started to fight and it was awful. I kept thinking of what would happen if I lost, and I kept praying to Jesus to give me strength. I kept calling on Jesus, saying his name. I don't know how long it went on, and we were all over the room. I won, of course, or I'd be dead.

"I called my roommate and asked him to help me clean up the room. The place was a mess. Ask him. It took us over an hour."

Actually he went on much longer than that, at least fifteen minutes, into great detail, evidently proud of his victories. When he finished, a silence fell upon the room and became awkward as it continued. Finally the group leader, who was Dixie's husband, asked the young Mexican: "What do you think? Do you want to move in?"

The young man was looking at the floor and he was frowning, and he said: "Let's see how the trial goes."

The leader said: "Okay. Then let's close the evening with a prayer. Jim?"

Jim, an older man, was standing behind my chair and I had not been aware of him. He asked us to stand and join hands, which we did, forming a circle, and he began a prayer of gratitude and praise that went on for several minutes. As he prayed, others in the room began to pray in tongues, the boy who had fought the devil, another black, the Oriental, a white boy who seemed quite young.

Tears streamed down this boy's face as he prayed, saying the name of Jesus over and over again. When the tongues began, the German shepherd dog, who had been asleep through all this, awoke and got up and began to pace about within our circle, nuzzling people. I happened to be standing at the door, and when the restless dog headed for me I thought he wanted to get out, so I broke the circle and stepped aside. But the dog remained within the group, moving about, nuzzling people.

The prayer ended. People began to leave. And that was the end of it all.

Duane Pederson said: "If you want to hear some *real* tongues, go out to Lyle Stennis's place." From Pederson's tone and expression, I took it that Lyle Stennis's place must have a wild flavor. Lyle Stennis's place was the Bethel Tabernacle in North Rodondo Beach. I phoned him and we made an appointment for seven o'clock at the church. I got there at six-thirty, to beat the crowd I expected would be there. Only a few young people were there, setting up for the evening service. I looked around. The church was bigger than it looked from the outside. Besides two sections of pews in the main area, there were rows of folding chairs to one side that apparently had been added to the building. A stage served as the sanctuary. Beneath it, I was told, was the baptismal pool where about a hundred people were baptized at a monthly service. Behind the stage was a room about forty-by-forty feet, the prayer room. Along the walls were wooden theatre seats; two rows of seats, back to back, ran down the middle of the room. Two girls were there, kneeling, using the seats as a prie-dieu, and one of them was praying in tongues softly. I wondered what Duane Pederson had in mind.

I went outside. Beyond the parking area was a structure that looked like a small motel. It turned out to be several small apartments for newcomers to the church to use temporarily until they got some roots. A boy appeared at one of the doors, came to me, and he asked: "Can I help you?"

"I'm waiting for Lyle Stennis," I said.
"He usually doesn't get here 'til seven-thirty."
"We have an appointment at seven."
"Oh. You a friend of his?"
"I'm meeting him for the first time."
"Oh."
"By the way, how will I recognize him?"
"He drives a gold Cadillac."
"Nice work."
"It was a present from somebody in the church that he helped."
"Are you a member of this church?"
"Yes. A new one. Just a few weeks."
"Where are you from?"

He was from Wisconsin, where he had been born and raised on a farm. His parents had expected that he would take over the farm one day, but he loathed farmwork and couldn't wait to get away. He got away about a year before, in his own car and with about four hundred dollars in savings. He was just eighteen. He arrived in California with every intention of finding a job and making a good life for himself. He rented a furnished room. With the expenses of his car, his room, his meals and an occasional movie, he ran through his savings in two months. He could not find a job. He had to sell his car. Friendless, he started going out to the Strip for some action. He got it. His room became a crash pad. His new friends introduced him to pot and poppers, and he found his own way to pills. He stopped looking for a job. His car money lasted four months, and a few weeks after that he was evicted from his room because he couldn't pay the rent. Now he went looking for crash pads. They were not hard to find, but he learned that if he stayed too long at one pad he would be expected to contribute to the larder. He had sold some of his clothes and the rest was stolen. He was flat broke. He tried panhandling and found it painfully degrading. So he took the advice of his new friends and turned to the only kind of work left for him: prostitution. His first experience with a man shocked him so severely that he was unable to go out on the streets unless he was high. Because he was high, he couldn't earn his fee, and usually he didn't get it. He took the final step: to earn his fee he sought out men who wanted him to be homosexually active. One afternoon on Hollywood Boulevard a man persuaded the boy to go all the way to the man's house at Rodondo Beach on the promise of plenty of drugs. The plentiful drug turned out to be heroin. The boy had already seen what heroin addiction had done to his new friends, including killing a few of them. As low as the boy felt he was, he nevertheless still wanted to live. He told the man that he would have to think this over and would do so on a walk around the block. He left the house and didn't go back.

Instead, he made his way to the beach. Hunger, weakness and his need for pills made him ill. He dropped to the sand and began to retch and vomit, and his whole body ached. He was only vaguely aware that some young people had come to him. He was only vaguely aware that they were asking him questions. He was only vaguely aware that they had helped him to his feet and to a car. Sometime later, he was only vaguely aware that the building into which they were guiding him was a church. They helped him up some stairs and into a small office and presented him to a short, stocky man and then left them alone. The room was spinning. The man's words reached the boy in a meaningless ruffle. But the boy did hear this:

"Jesus Christ is the only person who can help you now, son. Without Jesus you are sunk. If you try to go on living the way you are, you won't live much longer, son, take my word for it. But Jesus can help you. Jesus loves you. If you think you're hurting now, what do you think he's going through, watching you destroy yourself? He can save your life. He wants to. All you've got to do is ask. There's nothing else left for you. Yield to Jesus, son. Go ahead. Here, I'll help you. Kneel down. I'll pray with you."

The boy said to me: "It was like waking up out of a bad dream all of a sudden. First thing I knew was that I wasn't sick anymore. I didn't hurt so much. I was very tired, but I felt good. Something had hit me; I didn't know what it was, but I felt good. Another thing I couldn't figure out was what was I doing on my knees in front of a man, and him scratching my head?" He looked away and grinned to himself, then: "So I said: 'What happened?' And Lyle said: 'Jesus has given you the Baptism. You're cured. You're saved. You were praying in tongues.' I said: 'In what?' And Lyle said: 'Never mind. Praise the Lord! Go ahead, praise the Lord!' So I started talking, but I couldn't understand a word I was saying. This crazy sound kept coming out of me. And I felt so good. I felt so great. It was joy—that's the only word for it. Next thing I knew, I busted into tears."

There were tears in his eyes now, and he was smiling. I asked: "When did this happen?"

"About a month ago."

"What have you been doing with yourself since?"

"Not much. I was pretty run-down, y'know? I had lost a lot of weight. So Lyle had me move in with the married couple that's using that apartment for the time being," he said, pointing to the door where I had first seen him. "At first, I just slept and ate for a couple of weeks, going to church at night. Then I started Bible studies. When I learn enough, I'll start doing street-witnessing. And Lyle found me a job in a supermarket. I started last Monday. When I get some money together, maybe I'll take a place of my own or maybe I'll just move in with this couple when they find a permanent place. They're nice. We get along."

I said: "Sounds like you're staying around."

He laughed. "Only the United States Army could drag me away."

"The draft?"

"Yeah. Somewhere along the line I lost my draft card, so I wrote my mother and she went over to the draft board and got things fixed up. I'd hate leaving here, but the Bible says you should serve your country, so if I'm drafted I'll go."

"Have you been in touch with your parents all along?"

"No. And that was a wrong thing for me to do. The Bible says you should honor your mother and father. Everything's straightened out now, though."

"How do they feel about what's happened to you?"

"Well, they're glad that I'm practically living in a church," he said.

"Do they know about the drugs?"

"No. I just told them I had a rough year. I know that I'm through with that scene—Praise Jesus!—so why should I upset them with something that's ancient history? I'll witness the truth to other kids because I know I don't have anything new to tell them—except that they can be saved, as I was. But not my parents."

I asked: "Do your parents accept the fact that you're not going home?"

"Oh, yeah. They're happy enough that they know where they can always find me. In fact, they're coming out for Christmas. And my Dad said on the phone: 'Well, if you won't work for me, I guess the next best thing for you to do is work for the Lord.' " We laughed. The boy looked at me and asked: "What about you, mister? Are you working for the Lord?"

I said: "I hope so."

A gold Cadillac pulled in.

As I followed Lyle Stennis up to his office, we stopped at the foot of the stairs and looked into the prayer room. About fifteen people were there now, three or four boys, the rest girls. They were all praying in tongues, and a few of them were getting a little loud at it.

Stennis, then in his mid-forties, was a Kansan. While serving as a chaplain's assistant in the Army some twenty years previous, he felt called to the ministry. It was at this time, he told me, that he received the Baptism in the Holy Spirit. He took a correspondence course from an Oklahoma Bible college and subsequently was granted a certificate of ordination. He headed for California, for North Rodondo Beach and the Bethel Tabernacle because he felt that was where God wanted him. As a neon sign on the facade indicated, Bethel was a Full Gospel church—Pentecostal. Stennis told me that he had been preaching the Baptism, the gifts of the Spirit and the End Times all along.

In the mid-1960s, when the hippie movement was reaching its heights, Rodondo Beach was loaded with them, most of them high on drugs. Seeing this, Stennis realized that only God could help the kids, and he began going over to the beach to try to rap with them.

"I wasn't very successful," Stennis admitted to me. "I did manage to bring a few of them to the Lord, but I was too old. The kids wouldn't pay much attention to me. But then the Lord sent Breck Stevens to me."

Breck Stevens, a local boy, had, at fifteen, become a very successful dope pusher, with two hundred thousand dollars in the bank. Then he got caught and was sent up. He went through cold turkey by himself, and in the wake of it he realized that he had managed to make a thorough mess out of his life at an early age. Breck had not been a religious boy, obviously, but he was aware that God existed, and he knew now that God was all he had. He prayed: "Lord, unless I'm already doomed to spend most of my life behind bars, you'd better show me what you want me to do." The only answer he sensed to the prayer was a desire to read the Bible. As he began to read the Bible more and more, Breck also began to pray more and more, and gradually he became aware of what he wanted. It was while Breck Stevens was praying in his cell one night that he received the Baptism.

In April, 1968, Breck Stevens, at seventeen, got out of jail, and his first stop was the first church he saw. Bethel Tabernacle. He told Lyle Stennis about himself, and he said: "Reverend, I used to push dope, but now I want to push Jesus. If I can get through to the kids on the beach, can we come here to church?"

"You definitely can," Stennis said.

That evening, Breck was back with his first ten kids.

Stennis told me: "This is Breck's church now. I'm just the janitor. And I thank God."

The church changed rapidly. At the time, the congregation numbered over two hundred, mostly adults, and although they were vigorously Pentecostal they weren't prepared for the athletics the youngsters brought into the place. Breck Stevens, a small, lean, attractive young man, was a bundle of nerves. He spent all day on the beach, recruiting, and then, just so none of his prospects would waver, led a march on the church every evening. At first, Lyle Stennis led the service and gave the sermon, letting Breck tell his story just before the blessing and the altar call. Stennis found that Breck could take two hours to tell his story unless somebody shut him up, and yet this was the most exciting part of the meeting time after time. The kids sat at the edge of their seats, all attention, calling out "Yeah, man!" and "Praise the Lord!" and "Right on!" as Breck rocked back and forth in a one-step at the podium or walked quickly about the stage waving his arms. And the response to the altar call was like the response to a chow call at a Marine camp. Before long, Stennis dropped his sermon. Before long, the portrait of the congregation changed to ninety percent kids.

Because most of the kids came from somewhere else, a lot of them, when they felt sufficiently spiritually strong, went home and joined up with the Jesus People in their own communities. And, as I found out, there are Jesus People everywhere. But a lot of the kids stayed, maybe because they liked the town or the area, mostly because they liked the church and Stennis and Breck. This meant finding places for them to live. Stennis got on the phone. Before long, home-owners who had rented space to the kids and learned they were all right were on the phone to Stennis, letting him know when they had room for more. It also meant finding jobs for the kids. Again Stennis got on the phone. Again, it wasn't long before employers who had jobs for youngsters who weren't skilled at much, but who were willing to work hard at anything they could get, were on the phone to Stennis.

"So that's what I do around here," Stennis told me, joking. "I run an employment office and a renting agency. Breck runs the church."

I asked Stennis what his feelings were about the permanence of the Movement, and he said: "Well, some of the young people you'll see here tonight have been here almost from the beginning, and that's three years. I don't think that shows any signs of flightiness. The kids are settling down, getting married, having children, and some of the boys are moving into pretty good jobs. But the church is the center of their lives. Many of them are here every night. Their whole day is a witnessing experience. One thing I like a lot about them is their concern for old people. There are a lot of retired people in this area, shut-ins. The kids find out about them, visit them, do their housework, their shopping, read to them. An elderly person around here who gets sick doesn't even have to call us for help. The kids hear about it somehow and go over there to help out. Things like that convince me that the Movement is here to stay. After all, Pentecostalism has been around a long time. All it needed was young people to bring it to life."

I said: "Without mentioning any names, one of your friends gave me the impression that things got pretty wild around here. Sounds peaceful to me."

He went to the door and opened it. Up from the prayer room came a positive gale of tongues. He said: "Give them a few more minutes and we won't be able to hear each other."

I asked: "Is it all for real?"

"Ask God."

Stennis told me that one girl, upon receiving the Baptism during a church service, broke out in a language that seemed to be legitimate tongues, but a woman near her said: "That girl is speaking perfect Italian." Stennis said to me: "If the Holy Spirit wanted this girl to speak perfect Italian, there had to be a reason for it." Evidently there was. The church supports forty teams of missionaries —colonizers, more correctly—who have settled in Southern states and foreign countries to evangelize their communities. This girl joined a team that went to Italy.

Generosity was another characteristic which Stennis said the youngsters exhibited upon becoming Christians. "We don't have crash pads," he said, "but the married couples are always willing to take in new converts for a few weeks when we don't have room for them next door. Last month, two bus loads of kids from Fresno came down to share with us for a weekend, and doors were opened for them all over town. Also, the kids support the church better than the adults did. The collections are much better.

A much higher percentage of the kids tithe than did the adults. These young people care less for material things than their parents did."

It was getting harder to hear him.

I asked him how he thought this whole thing had come about, and he said: "It's the work of the Lord. That's the first thing. The Lord saw what was happening to our kids. The hippie culture. Drugs. The highest venereal disease rate in history. Now, these kids you're going to see tonight, if they had been their present ages ten years ago, they would have joined the Peace Corps. They're good kids; they wanted to do good; they started out good. But they grew up on a war nobody can explain to them. They grew up on exposés of corruption in government and business. They grew up on a soaring divorce rate. They grew up watching their parents lose more workdays to alcoholism than to the common cold. And nobody was doing anything about the mess. The churches certainly weren't making much of an effort. So the kids tried demonstrations and strikes and running away, but all that didn't change anything. So the kids dropped out. We entered the hippie era. Well, I believe that the Lord watched all this and decided that the time had come to send the Holy Spirit. And now we have the Jesus Movement."

"And we're in the End Times?"

"We are."

We were, in fact. Stennis had to get ready for the evening service. I went downstairs. The prayer room was packed. There was a person kneeling at every seat. Others knelt in the middle of the room. Some were standing, their arms waving over their heads. They were all praying in tongues, and the place was in an uproar.

A girl stepped up to me. She asked: "Can you pray in tongues?"

I said: "No."

She asked: "Do you want me to teach you how?"

I said: "No, thanks."

So they weren't all for real.

People were beginning to arrive for the service, so I went to the main door to watch them come in. They were mostly girls. Few of the boys had beards; few had long hair. There were several older people, in their forties and fifties, mostly women. Everybody was so friendly. Everybody whose eyes met mine smiled and said hello. A couple of young men gave me a handshake—the straight kind, although they gave each other the Movement's grip. The place was starting to fill up. I took a seat.

Lyle Stennis came out on the stage with two older men and a young man who turned out to be Breck Stevens. Stevens had a straight haircut and he had no beard. He was wearing slacks, a regular white shirt, opened at the collar, no tie, the sleeves rolled up. He effused charm, joy and attractiveness. He looked like the boy next door when the boy next door used to look like a boy next door.

First Stennis made some announcements, including the news that the pianist was out sick and that unless someone in the house volunteered to play the piano the singing that night would be accompanied only by himself on drums. No volunteers. He also had a couple of jobs offers, but apparently nobody in the house needed one. He identified the two men on stage as visiting clergymen.

Then Breck Stevens took over. The place perked up right away. Stevens spoke very rapidly, often repeating words, gesturing, moving about a lot. He began with: "Hi. Good evening. Good evening everybody. Anybody get the Spirit today? Anybody get the Spirit? Anybody got any news? Anybody got anything to share with us? Let's sing a few songs. Let's sing a few nice songs. And then if anybody has anything to share with us—if anybody wants to tell us what Jesus is doing for him—I want you to come up here and share it. Okay?"

The singing was robust, Stennis providing a steady beat on the drums on the stage. We stood during much of the singing. If the lyrics said something like: "I raise my arms up to the Lord," up went arms throughout the church. There was a great deal of clapping. When the thing really got going, youngsters moved into the aisles and started dancing with such vigorous hip-swinging that I expected them to churn up a hurricane. I was beginning to understand what Duane Pederson had meant. Again, as at Calvary Chapel, I was prepared not to know the hymns and so, sitting or standing, I did not pick up a hymnal. Anyway, I wanted to watch and listen. But again, the people around me were always either leaning to me with their hymnals or handing me one. As at Calvary, most of the people seemed to know all the hymns by heart. The singing and dancing and waving and clapping went on for an hour; and though I had been merely an observer through most of it, I was exhausted.

Then several people went to the stage to share. The first, a girl who said her name was Dorothy and that she was nineteen, said: "I just got the Baptism tonight in the prayer room. I feel so wonderful. Now I know that Jesus really loves me because he gave me the Baptism." Jeff, seventeen, said: "I always used to feel strange. I always felt bad inside. I used to blame it on the drugs, but even when I cut down I still felt rotten. A Christian friend of mine told me that the problem was that I didn't know Jesus. My friend said I should start praying. I tried praying but nothing happened. My friend brought me here a couple of times, and I enjoyed myself but I just didn't feel part of it. So one night my friend said that he could pray me into the Baptism if I really wanted it, and I told him go ahead. We did it on the beach. I knelt down and he put his hands on my head and prayed in tongues. It didn't take five minutes. The Spirit hit me like a ton of bricks. I fell right over. Then I started to pray in tongues. It was terrific. I never felt so great. It was funny. My friend and I were both crying and hugging each other. People thought we were crazy. Another thing, I knew I was through with drugs. I just knew I wouldn't need them anymore. I had some pills on me and I ran right down to the water and I threw them into the ocean. That was over three months ago, and I haven't even felt the need for drugs since then. All I need is Jesus." Throughout this witnessing, people in the congregation called out "Praise the Lord!" and "Praise Jesus!"

One of two crewmen of a Swedish freighter caught in port by the West Coast dock strike said: "We came ashore one night to look for some girls. We found some. But they were Jesus People, and they brought us here to church. We thought they had tricked us, but we had such a good time here that we kept coming back every night on our own. One night last week when we were praying together aboard ship, we both got the Baptism. We're very happy about it, and we promise you that before the ship gets back to Sweden we are going to convert every member of the crew." Scott, seventeen, said: "I used to be on witchcraft, and I thought it was the right thing for me to do. But then I started noticing that everything in my life was goofed up. I was always putting my trust in other people. I found out what happens when you put your trust in another person—they drop you. So I wondered if I was serving the wrong Master. About a year ago, I turned to Jesus. I went to several different churches, but nothing happened. Then I came here and I found my Jesus. Nobody has to tell me anymore what a friend I've got in Jesus. I know he'll never drop me, I know he'll never disappoint me, I know he loves me, and my life is all right now." Kathy, fifteen, said: "Two years ago, my boyfriend turned me on to drugs. Then I met this woman, and I started turning on with her. Both my boyfriend and my girlfriend were always telling me that they loved me. I believed them, and so I felt that everything we were doing was all right. Now I know it was just the Devil deceiving me. I used to stay with my girlfriend a few days at a time and nobody ever thought anything of it, y'know, because it was a woman. But one day my brother came over unexpectedly and, well, he saw through everything. My brother comes to this church, and he said he wouldn't tell Mother anything if I would go to church with him every night for a month, and I had to say yes. It took ten days. I was in the prayer room with my brother and he was praying in tongues and holding my hands, and I got the Spirit. I kicked all my hang-ups in that minute, and all I want to say now is: 'Jesus, keep that door open. There are a lot of kids like me who need you.' "

There were others.

Then Breck Stevens gave his sermon.

He went on for over an hour. He was interesting, amusing and effective. He was also very athletic, moving about constantly. He must have covered five miles. His theme was that a Christian was not a coward. At first, he talked in terms of the End Times, of the persecution which Christians will have to suffer during this period, and then he became more pertinent to the present day. He said: "A Christian does not burn up his draft card. A Christian does not go to Canada. A Christian serves his country when his country needs him." With that, he seemed to wipe out the total value of the individual conscience.

The Sunday morning I attended services at Calvary Chapel, Chuck Smith announced: "Lonnie will be back sometime next week." A murmur of pleasure rose from the congregation. Duane Pederson told me that Lonnie Frisbee had joined the Jesus Movement at one of Pederson's rallies, he had been trained by Pederson's people, and Pederson had ordained him. Frisbee, in his early twenties and married, worked out of Newport Beach, but he was also in charge of the young people's programs at Calvary Chapel.

Duane Pederson also told me that when I met Chuck Smith I would be meeting a man full of love, and I told Smith this as he led me into his office on a Wednesday afternoon. Smith smiled and said: "Duane is a good friend." The office was small but attractively decorated. Smith was dressed casually, and he seemed to be a much more subdued man than the vibrant preacher I'd heard ten days before.

Smith said he was as amazed as everyone else by the soaring growth of his congregation. A native of the Los Angeles area and educated in local schools and seminaries, he was ordained in 1948. He said: "When we moved out here two years ago, I told myself I'd be happy if I got a congregation of three hundred people. Now, five thousand are here every Sunday. Our growth appears to be about five percent a week. We're going to expand the church, but I doubt that we'll ever get it big enough to accommodate everybody."

I asked: "Do you think it's because you preach the Holy Spirit?"

"I have always preached the Holy Spirit," he said. "I think it's because the Holy Spirit himself is busier. This is his hour."

"The End Times?"

"We're in them."

I said: "I expected to see some Street People in your congregation, but I don't recall seeing any."

He said: "You saw a lot of people who used to be Street People, if you're talking about hippies and addicts. But they are Christians now. They know that cleanliness is next to godliness. They knew that a Christian is supposed to work and earn his own living. They know that a Christian is supposed to be married to the mother of his children. They know that a Christian is supposed to go to church."

I asked: "Then how come so many Jesus People, including some of the leaders I've interviewed, are so anti-church?"

"They have a right to be," he said firmly. "More churches are closed to the Jesus People than are open to them. As far as I know, I was the first pastor around here to go out after the Jesus People and invite them into my church. You see, a lot of pastors feel that the Jesus Movement is too Pentecostal Church oriented, and the reason this may seem true is that the Jesus People are over-emphasizing tongues. Speaking or praying in tongues has always been regarded as the Pentecostals' area, and a lot of pastors feel that if they let their people turn loose on tongues their churches will lose their Lutheranism or Presbyterianism or any 'ism' involved. Well, I don't feel that way. Although Paul told people not to overdo tongues, he did urge people to seek the Baptism and its gifts, and I go along with Paul. We don't allow tongues during our services, but on the other hand I'll do everything I can to help a person receive the Baptism. And I've done it thousands of times."

I said: "I heard tongues during your service last Sunday."

He frowned. "Well, you shouldn't have. People know my policy on that. We feel that if the minister doing the teaching and the preaching has had the anointment, then God is talking through him, and it would be inconsistent to have him be interrupted by someone in the congregation who is compelled to give a so-called message in tongues. I believe in the gift of prophecy, of course, but prophecy is only meaningful when someone is present who can interpret it. God knows about these things: He would not interrupt a religious service with a prophecy unless He knew there was someone present who could interpret it."

"Has a prophecy ever been interpreted here during one of your services?"

"No."

We talked about the communes supported by Calvary Chapel in the immediate area and in Oregon and of the evangelizers moving out from these places to settle in new communities. I asked: "Is it your idea, then, to send Jesus People out across the country and have them become part of the society where they settle down?"

"I hope not," he said. "I think society stinks. Our prayer is that the Jesus People will *convert* the communities where they settle down."

"Society stinks?"

"Yes," he said. "We don't have a pollution problem by accident. We don't have a drug problem just because of the pressures of peer groups. We don't have wars just because there is no other way to settle disputes. We don't have corruption in government just because there are weaknesses in our form of democracy. People—society—have brought these problems upon us because people are greedy and materialistic and deceitful and un-loving."

That settled that. I asked: "But as the number of Jesus People increases, until we are all Jesus People, won't the situation change and improve?"

"It's too late," Smith said. "As soon as God let Israel become a nation again, He put us on notice that we have about thirty or forty years left."

"Then why bother?"

"Because the Christians who can keep their faith during the Last War will be able to live in a world ruled by Jesus Christ for a thousand years of peace and joy. That's worth bothering about. As Christians, it's the duty of Jesus People to strengthen the faith of as many people as possible so that they can resist the Anti-Christ when he shows up, and that's what this is all about."

I asked: "Does the thought of all the horror that's just ahead of us depress you?"

He said: "Absolutely not! Jesus is coming soon. For a Christian, that's the happiest thought in the world!"

It was a Wednesday and, that night, Lonnie Frisbee was to conduct his first Young People's Bible Study since returning from Europe. The service was to begin at seven-thirty; Chuck Smith warned me that the kids would start showing up at five. It was around five when my visit with Smith ended and, sure enough, a couple of dozen youngsters had already gathered in the church. I went to dinner and was back by six-thirty. The church was half-filled. Although there was still room in the pews, a lot of the kids preferred the floor, sitting down in the aisles and in the open space in front of the sanctuary. By seven, there wasn't an unoccupied inch in the church. To get a better view and have freedom of movement, I had taken a folding chair against the wall in the foyer at the back of the church. By seven, the foyer was packed with kids, some on folding chairs, most on the floor, and the only way I could have moved about was with the gift of flight. By seven-thirty, the patio was jammed with the overflow.

They were a good-looking bunch of kids. A few of the girls had long dresses; a few of the boys had long hair. Several Orientals were present, but I didn't see any Negroes. The rest of the kids looked like young actors answering an open call for extras in an Andy Hardy movie. They all seemed to know each other. They greeted each other with embraces and kisses and the Jesus People handshake. The roar of the conversation was deafening. If I had been told that this was a class reunion of kids who had not seen each other for five years, I would have believed it, but I knew perfectly well that most of these kids had been here last night and would be here tomorrow night and that this great outpouring of joy was part of their thing.

Around seven-thirty, four or five young people came out onto the raised area of the sanctuary, and for a moment I thought they must have wandered into the wrong place. With one exception, they looked like caricatures of Jesus People—the boys with the long hair and beards and old clothes, the girls with their long hair pulled tightly back, long dresses, no make-up. The exception turned out to be Lonnie Frisbee. His full growth of brown hair made his head look bigger than it was; his full growth of brown beard made his face seem smaller than it was. He was wearing a two-piece, Chinese-type suit that was white but which picked up flashes of pink and amber from overhead lights as he moved about. The sight of him silenced the crowd.

Frisbee stepped to a microphone and raised his right arm in the Jesus People salute, index finger pointing, and he said: "Praise the Lord!"

A forest of right arms shot into the air, index fingers pointing, heads tilted slightly to the right for some reason, and there was a roar of: "PRAISE THE LORD!"

Then Frisbee said: "Hi. I love every one of you." He had a thin, high, boyish voice. "It's wonderful to be back," he said. "We had a wonderful trip. We'll tell you about it later. First, let's praise Jesus with some singing."

The singing went on for an hour and a half, and it was terrific. The only person who used a hymnal was Frisbee himself, and he seemed to be using one just to pick out the next song. Some of the songs were rousing, some beautifully plaintive. One hymn—"Arky, Arky"—having to do with Noah's Ark, was perky fun, with the animals coming aboard in "twosies, twosies," and it involved a great deal of gesturing, all of which the kids knew by heart. There were several stanzas, and in the chorus there was a point where the kids clapped their hands once and gave the Jesus People salute, and they did this each time with such open and carefree joy that I found myself looking forward to it and laughing when they did it. Another hymn—"We Are One In The Spirit"—had a haunting melody and contained a moving thought. The last line went something like: "And they'll know that we are Christians by our love, by our love, oh, they'll know that we are Christians by our love." The kids sang it with such quiet sincerity and warmth that each time I heard it—three times that night, and other nights in other places—I found myself thinking: "I believe you."

Then some chairs were brought out on the stage around nine o'clock, and Frisbee announced that we were now going to be told about his trip. Some time previous, some Swedish Christians had come to California to investigate the Jesus Movement for themselves, and they were so impressed by what they saw at Calvary Chapel that they invited Frisbee and his wife and two other couples to go to Sweden and conduct services there. Evidently, the trip had been a huge success. One by one, the six youngsters gave us their impressions. They had drawn big crowds wherever they appeared. They appeared on radio and television. Newspaper articles about them appeared on front pages—Frisbee held up a few samples. People stopped them on the street for autographs. Thousands responded to altar calls. The spirituality of the country had impressed them. They said things like: "You could really feel the Holy Spirit at work in Sweden. I could tell that those people are really looking for the Lord. I'll bet that Sweden becomes the first country in Europe to give itself over completely to the Lord." They had received invitations to appear to other European countries but did not have the time or funds on this trip. They intended to go back.

On the way home, they ran into some unpleasantness. Frisbee said:

"We made a stop-over in London, and they told us there was going to be a big Christian rally that night at Albert Hall and they asked us to take part in it. Well, we had the time, and we knew it was a big honor, so we said yes. It was terrific. The place was packed and there was television and a lot of famous Englishmen were there, ready to tell how they came to give their lives to the Lord and how they got the Spirit. Well, the thing was going along for a while, when all of a sudden this riot broke out. It was homosexuals. Most of them were in the balcony, but they were on the main floor, too, and they started throwing eggs and tomatoes at the people on the stage. Eggs and tomatoes were splattering all over the place. And the homosexuals were screaming that Christianity was discriminating against them. They said the churches wouldn't accept them as Christians and homosexuals at the same time.

"They began to run down the aisles and onto the stage, and some of them were in drag. And they grabbed the microphones and demanded their rights, and they started to argue with the rest of us on the stage. I told one of them that the Bible says they are an abomination. The Bible says that God has given up on them. I told him he didn't have to be a homosexual, that God would change him if he asked. I told him where the Bible says that Paul wrote to the Corinthians about the homosexuals in Corinth who were changed when they got the Baptism. So I told him that he should pray for the Baptism and he would be changed. He said he didn't want to be changed, and he told me to go to hell. I told him that he'd be going to hell himself, and soon. I told him that the Bible says that one of the signs of the End Times was that more and more men would be having sex with each other and more and more women would be having sex with each other, and he said that was what he was looking forward to.

"It was awful, everybody arguing and hollering. Somebody sent for the police, and then there was all that noise as the homosexuals were being arrested and taken away. That broke up the meeting, of course. The people told us they would try to arrange another meeting some other night, but our time was up and we had to head for home. But it was awful."

Throughout this, there were occasional gasps from the kids in the church, and a few laughs.

The thought had not occurred to me that, on this trip, I would run into the subject of homosexuality as much as I did. The subject usually came up with the leaders, but always as a sign of the End Times. But numerous young men casually referred to their homosexual experiences as they told me the stories of their lives. Some said they had hustled men in order to support themselves and their drug habits. Others said they participated in the sex simply because it was part of the scene. A few said they had already accepted themselves as homosexuals at the time they experienced the Baptism, and being changed was not the reason they had sought the Baptism but a result of it. Now I was beginning to wonder if this openness was evidence of the generation gap, since the days of my own youth when even the best of friends never admitted to each other that they ever masturbated. I also wondered if it was evidence of the permissive society I'd heard so much about—anything goes. Then I came to look upon it in another light. It seemed to me that these young men were merely admitting to me that their lives had become caught up in the signs of the End Times, of which homosexuality was just one part, and now that they had received the Baptism they could look backward without shame and forward without fear.

We sang some more hymns. I never did get "Arky, Arky" down, but I enjoyed knowing that we were all one in the Spirit.

Then Lonnie Frisbee announced a communion service. It was now ten o'clock and some people were leaving. For the communion service, long loaves of sliced whole wheat bread were brought onto the stage, opened, and the slices were piled on wooden trays. Then ushers carried the bread up the aisles, giving a few slices to the person sitting at the end of each pew. People broke off bite-sized pieces as the slices were passed along. By the time a piece of bread reached me, out in the foyer, I figured that about thirty people had already handled it. But my Catholic conscience bothered me more than hygiene. I knew what receiving communion meant in my church, and I was not sure that I was supposed to go along with this. I decided to wait and see how things went.

The prayer Lonnie Frisbee said before the bread was to be eaten stressed the fellowship of Christianity and the commemorative aspect of the ceremony itself. I could go along with that. I ate the piece of bread. I noticed that many people fed the bread to each other.

Then Frisbee announced that the liquid portion of the ceremony would be served to all who wished to go forward and drink from the chalice. Many people went forward. I wondered whether the liquid was wine or grape juice. Then I remembered where I was and I remembered how young some of the kids were, and I realized it couldn't be wine. So I decided that I had carried fellowship far enough. I had never liked grape juice.

A lot of people left, and I was able to go into the church and find a seat. There were still about a hundred people there. We sang some hymns. Then Frisbee announced: "Now we are going to have a healing service and I will baptize you in the Holy Spirit. But first I have to say something. Don't be disappointed if nothing seems to happen to you tonight. Sometimes these things take a few days. But I know there will be healings and I know there will be Baptisms. Okay, come on up."

Some people went forward.

At the far end of the pew in which I sat, four girls were talking intently to a fifth girl with them. All I could perceive from my distance was that this girl seemed uncertain about something. Suddenly her expression changed, and she got up and went forward. As Frisbee prayed over each person, he placed his hands on the individual's head. From my distance, I could not determine whether Frisbee was using tongues. When he finished and moved on, the individual turned and went back to his seat. I could not observe anything different about the person.

Then Frisbee prayed over this girl. When she turned, she fairly flew up the aisle to her friends. Tears were streaming down her face, and yet she was beaming. As her friends gathered around her, she kept putting her hands to her face, wiping away the tears, and she kept exclaiming softly: "Oh! Oh! Oh, oh!" And she could not stand still. Her friends embraced her and kissed her and tried to calm her, but soon they were all weeping and laughing and kissing and embracing each other, and one of them said: "Let's get out of here before we get any worse."

So something had happened.

5

In The Beginning...

The leaders of the Jesus Movement kept assuring me that nothing new was happening. What was happening, they said, was that something which had been lost had now been found again. As it happened, the re-discovery was made independently, at different places and at different times, by the men and women who came to constitute the leadership of the Jesus Movement. It also happened that many of these individuals met and became friends. They cooperated with each other, conducting joint services, but they remained independent. No new church was formed. On the other hand, existing churches were being extensively re-formed because of the fact that the Movement had come into existence. It was true that many churches had closed their doors to the Jesus People, but this was mostly out of fear and ignorance. The time came, however, when the people on the inside of the closed doors began seeking the very things which the Jesus People had offered them. And it was nothing new.

The Jesus People believe that they are today's heirs of certain aspects of Christianity which have always been practiced, somewhere, in one way or another, ever since there were Christians. Paul told the Corinthians not to go overboard with tongues in public ceremonies, and the Early Church discouraged the use of it at all. But, surely, this wasn't the end of it. And, surely, the Jesus People were not the resumption of it, less than ten years ago. As long as men have had Bibles, men have known about the Gifts of the Holy Spirit, and surely the Holy Spirit has not been waiting around for what may be the End Times to make his presence known. The Jesus People believe that if God has a plan for the world, then He has a plan, and it has been unfolding steadfastly all along. If there has been little evidence over the centuries of the role of the Holy Spirit in that plan, then perhaps men have not understood that role or recognized it, and so few records were made of it and, until lately, the Holy Spirit remained the neglected member of the Trinity. Lately, however, men have been trying to compile a record, and a couple of events have come to light which, the Jesus People claim, bring into perspective their own position in God's plan.

Late in 1900, Charles F. Parham, a Methodist minister working in the Midwest, started to grow discouraged with his ministry. A devout student of the Bible, he had read often of the vigorous and effective missionary work of the Apostles, and he knew that nothing like this was happening to him. He could only conclude that there was something in the Bible that he was missing completely. At first, he thought that he could solve his problem through further study, but then he realized that he would need outside help, the kind of help that could be derived from exchanging views with others schooled in the Bible. Out of these broodings came an idea to open a house of studies where people already advanced in their knowledge of the Bible could live together as they pursued, through study, prayer and discussion, the ingredient that seemed to have gone out of Christianity, the ingredient that had made Christianity so alive, so vibrant, so gripping to the first people who heard its messages from the Apostles.

Parham was able to obtain in Topeka, Kansas, a mansion that had been abandoned by its owner. His next question was: Who shall be the other students? His first plan was to invite Bible scholars from universities and large churches, but he rejected this. He realized that such men probably were not at liberty for this kind of project, that as experts they probably were too firmly opinionated to have much room for curiosity, and that, because he was just an ordinary minister, they probably wouldn't pay much attention to him, anyway. So Parham simply made a public announcement of what he was trying to do, and then he sat back to see if anybody would show up.

Before the week was out, he had forty students, young men like himself, men who knew their Bible but who also knew they were not deriving from it all of their spiritual rewards that they knew were there. Many arrived with their wives and children, plus their household effects. In a way, the old mansion became the first Jesus People commune.

The study, prayer and discussions began. Out of it all came a general agreement that the ingredient missing in the Christianity of the day was a prevalence of the Baptism in the Holy Spirit, if it was occurring at all. And yet the Bible put such emphasis on the Baptism. John the Baptist told people that he was baptizing them with water but that someone who would come after him would baptize people with the Spirit. That someone was Jesus Christ. During the last months of his ministry, Jesus spoke increasingly to the Apostles about the Holy Spirit. After his resurrection, he told the Apostles to remain together in Jerusalem and that he would send the Holy Spirit to them. The terrified Apostles were praying together in the Upper Room when they were suddenly filled with the Spirit. This was the Pentecost. Catholics have maintained that the Christian Church came into being at the Last Supper, when Jesus instituted the sacrament of Holy Communion, but Protestants have generally held that the Church was born upon the Pentecost. Either way, if the Apostles derived spiritual solace and strength from the Eucharist, it was the Holy Spirit who exhilarated them with the spiritual courage to go out and evangelize a hostile world, each of them, except John the beloved Apostle, eventually suffering a violent execution for the sake of the Lord.

But the Pentecost experience did not appear to be intended solely for the Apostles. Paul hadn't been in the Upper Room, and yet he had the Baptism. Also, it would not have been necessary for Paul to admonish the Corinthians about the misuse of the gifts of the Holy Spirit if the Baptism had been a rarity among them. And the Epistles referred to the occurrence of the Baptism in other places, and most of the time the Baptism was accompanied by the gift of tongues.

Why, then, the Parham group wondered, had it all stopped? They came to the conclusion that it had not stopped at all but that it had been stopped, through the discouragement of Paul, through the exaggeration of this discouragement by the Early Church, and then through neglect over the centuries. True, the Catholic Church—and later the Lutheran Church and Episcopal Church—had a sacrament of confirmation, the baptism of the Holy Spirit referred to three times in the Book of Acts, but the baptism itself was regarded as the gift—the gift of stronger faith—and the gifts which Paul discussed with the Corinthians—tongues, interpretation of tongues, healing, prophecy, the others—were evidently neglected. It was also true that many Catholic saints had suddenly acquired the ability to speak in an unknown language; but though it was a language that was unknown to them, it was still a known language, the language of another land where the saint had never been. Furthermore, when the saint spoke in the language, he knew what he was saying, and he also knew what was being said when someone of that language spoke to him. The difficulty with the glossolalia, as Paul pointed out, was that the person speaking usually had no idea what he was saying, and nobody else near him had any idea, either, unless someone was present who had the gift to interpret. Paul therefore instructed that praying in tongues should be private. Even so, he admitted that he probably prayed in tongues more than anyone else. It was this that convinced the Parham group that there had to be a spiritual good in tongues, and they sought the Baptism.

To recreate the circumstances of the Pentecost, Parham set apart a room on the second floor of the mansion as the Upper Room. The room was never empty. Around the clock, students were in there, praying for the Baptism. Days passed. Weeks passed. Nothing happened. Then, toward the end of the year, one of the students, Agnes Ozman, went to Parham with an observation she had made. It seemed, she said, that each time there was a reference in the Epistles to the Baptism there was also a reference to the laying of hands upon the person seeking the Baptism. Now she wondered if the laying of hands, a gesture involved in religious acts throughout the Bible, was part of the Baptism procedure. She asked Parham to pray with her that way.

Tradition has it that at 7 p.m. on New Year's Eve, 1900, kneeling at prayer in the mansion's Upper Room, Parham praying with her, his hands upon her head, Agnes Ozman prayed in tongues for the first time. In her own account of the experience, however, Agnes Ozman said the event occurred around 11 p.m. on January 1, 1901. No matter. It happened. It happened in front of witnesses. Although, for almost a century, there had been reports from here and there of people praying in tongues, this was the first such event to be witnessed and documented before, during and after the Baptism occurred. For Pentecostalism, this was the beginning.

Within a few days, practically everybody living in the mansion, including Parham, received the Baptism. Word spread through Topeka about the strange sounds emanating from the house, and there were inquiries. Visitors were invited to attend prayer meetings. One visitor was a man who had been born and raised in Bohemia; and after he heard Agnes Ozman pray in tongues, he told her that she had spoken perfect Bohemian. Agnes Ozman did not have any idea where Bohemia was.

Several leaders of the Jesus Movement told me: "When it comes to the Baptism, as important as the gifts are, the fruits of the gifts are even more important." This was what happened at Topeka. The people found that their prayers, whether in tongues or English, became a more fulfilling spiritual exercise. Their prayers also seemed to be more efficacious. And, somehow, the people became more sensitive to guidance. Another thing, the Bible became more precious to them; passages that had been difficult to comprehend before now made sense. Most important was their awareness, their clear awareness, of the presence of the Lord in their daily lives. They felt a great joy, a great freedom, a great love.

They had to tell the world. They went in a group to Kansas City where they witnessed on the streets, gave interviews to the press, and took their message to the church leaders. They ran into a brick wall. The church leaders denounced them, the press ridiculed them, and the people on the streets thought they were all batty. When their money was gone and they saw they could proceed no further in Kansas City, they returned to Topeka, only to find that the mansion they had rented had been sold. There was nothing the students could do but go back to their own homes, each pledging to continue to work for the Lord, preaching the Baptism.

Parham couldn't get a job. The bad publicity he had received in Kansas City closed all pulpits to him. For three years, he wandered around the Midwest, preaching on street corners and supporting his family on whatever odd jobs he could get. He preached what he called "the full Gospel," not excluding any controversial parts of the

Bible, like the Baptism, which a lot of ministers avoided because they didn't understand it. In 1903, Parham settled at El Dorado Springs, Missouri, a health spa. Every day, he went to the springs to preach to the people about the healings of Jesus Christ, a healing he said was available to them through faith. Some people became interested, and they started gathering at Parham's home in the evenings for prayer meetings. He would put his hands upon them and pray, and some of them were healed.

Among those who felt they had benefited from Parham's prayers was Mrs. Mary Arthur, of Galena, Kansas. Surgery had failed to correct an eye condition that was threatening her vision, but after Charles Parham had prayed over her she experienced a distinct improvement. Returning to Galena, Mrs. Arthur told her friends what had happened to her, with the result that Parham was invited to Galena to conduct services in Mrs. Arthur's home. In just a few days of services, there was not room for everybody who wanted to attend, and so a warehouse had to be rented. Night after night, the place was packed with people who wanted to find out about the Baptism in the Holy Spirit, people who wanted the Baptism for themselves.

But Charles Parham sensed that this was not the ministry the Lord wanted him to pursue. A cult was developing around him, and this, he felt, was the wrong route. He was aware of a deep yearning to train other ministers in the ways of the Holy Spirit so that there could be a steadily increasing ministry in this area, and he accepted the yearning as guidance. For this reason, Parham remained at Galena only three months and then, in the fall of 1905, he moved on to Houston, Texas, and he opened another school. Because of the national publicity that had come out of Galena, the news that he had opened a training center for ministers quickly brought in applicants.

Among the applicants was W. S. Seymour, a Negro preacher. Upon finishing the course, Seymour was invited to preach a series of sermons at a Negro church in Los Angeles. His first sermon was so blatantly Pentecostal that the rest of the series was canceled. Virtually stranded, Seymour accepted an invitation from a Negro family to stay with them until he got his bearings, and Seymour began conducting prayer meetings in their home. On April 9, 1906, a boy who was present received the Baptism and started speaking in tongues. That same evening, six others received the Baptism. The news spread rapidly. The next night, the overflow filled the backyard of the old building, and people were getting the Baptism left and right. One night the crowd inside got so carried away by their spiritual athletics that the building actually collapsed. Miraculously, there were no injuries.

Looking around for a new place to worship, Seymour located an abandoned Baptist church at 312 Azusa Street, situated, in a rundown neighborhood, between a lumberyard and a livery stable. The building needed a lot of work, but there was a plethora of volunteers among the new Christians, and they quickly had the building in shape. And the building became famous all over the world. For that matter, people went there from all over the world, to attend the endless services, to watch the frenetic freaks, and then, many of them, to be caught up in the fervor and find themselves pleading for the Baptism. It was the spirit of the place that captured people. Seymour himself had little education and was hardly a dynamic speaker. Most of the time he remained aside, his head bowed, quietly praying in tongues, while the people sang full-blast and witnessed and spoke in tongues and prayed each other into the Baptism. Because of the involvement of the Holy Spirit, the activities at the church were described as "Pentecostal," and for the three years the revival lasted, people who had arrived as Baptists, Methodists, Catholics or what-have-you went home as Pentecostals.

And when they got home, the welcome mat was gone from their church doors. The staid, old-line churches wanted no part of this hand-clapping, dancing-in-the-aisles, gibbering-in-tongues hysteria. Rather than give up their new joy in worship, many of the new Pentecostals withdrew from their old churches and started their own prayer groups; and as the prayer groups increased in size and number and places of worship became necessary, the Pentecostals started their own churches.

For the sake of organization, the churches began to form into affiliations, and then the affiliations began to merge. For example, in 1907 the Association of Pentecostal Churches in America, a Northeastern group, merged with the Church of the Nazarene, to form the Pentecostal Church of the Nazarene. A year later, the Holiness Church of Christ, originating in Texas, joined this union. In 1915, the Pentecostal Mission, organized in Tennessee, also joined. By then, there were Pentecostals all over the world and many countries were moving toward their own national associations. In 1949, the World Conference of Pentecostal Fellowships was established, with its headquarters in Geneva, Switzerland. Its secretary-general was David du Plessis, a South African, whose family became Pentecostals in 1908—when du Plessis was eight—after attending services in Johannesburg given by two missionaries from Azusa Street. In the summer of 1960, David du Plessis visited John Sherrill's home at Mt. Kisco, New York, happening to arrive on the day the Sherrills were packing to move to Chappaqua. Du Plessis spent the day helping the Sherrills pack as he discussed with them his own experiences with the Baptism in the Holy Spirit, an experience which John was to have himself six months later.

Another event which seems to dovetail as part of the development of the Jesus People movement began as long ago as 1880 in the village of Kara Kala in Armenia, near the Turkish border. Presbyterian missionaries had evangelized the area and won many converts, some of whom had received the Spirit and spoke in tongues. Living in the village was an illiterate boy, eleven years old and of Russian parentage, and one day he felt guided to go on a week's fast. Before the week was out, the boy announced that he was experiencing a vision, and he asked for a pen and paper so he could write down what he was seeing. In perfect Russian, he wrote something like this: "All the Christians must leave this place. The Turks are coming, and they will kill the Christians because of their religion. There will be murder everywhere. The Christians must go." And then, without any schooling at all, he drew a map of where the Christians should go. The United States.

Nobody believed the boy. Just a few years before, in 1878, the Congress of Berlin had placed Armenia under the protection of the powerful Russian Empire, and there seemed little likelihood that the Turks would be so stupid or so audacious as to attack a country that could squash them like an ant. Even so, the elders of the church thought the document was of interest because it had been written by a boy who could not read his own words.

Among those who did not believe the boy and his vision was another boy, Demos Shakarian, fifteen, the son of a dairy farmer. The boy became a dairy farmer, too, and he married. Over the years, his wife presented him with five daughters. Now, there was a belief in the town that if a man did not have a son it was because God was punishing him for some reason. Shakarian could not imagine what in the world he had done.

On May 25, 1891, Shakarian's wife was being visited by her brother, who had received the Baptism, and they spent part of the afternoon reading the Bible aloud. Suddenly the brother interrupted himself and said: "God has just spoken to me. Exactly one year from this day, you will give birth to a son." When Shakarian's wife told him about this, he just laughed. But he made a mental note of the date. On May 25, 1892, Demos Shakarian became the father of a son. He made a mental note of the date. He did not know what to make of it, but after that he didn't laugh when people said God had just spoken to them.

Twenty years passed. The boy who'd had the vision was now a middle-aged man, still unable to read or write, but still he held that his vision had been valid, and now he was telling people: "The time is soon. The Lord has told me. We should all get out of here." This time, there seemed to be some practical evidence to support the man. Armenians living in Turkish cities were being forced into a ghetto existence; their businesses were being confiscated, and Turkey was building up its army.

This time, Demos Shakarian decided not to take any chances. He sold his farm and moved where the boy—the man, now—had said. America. He chose to settle in California and, as hundreds of other Armenian families were doing, he settled in the Joaquin Valley. He bought a dairy farm. When his son—Isaac—was grown and married, he also became a dairy farmer. Isaac had a son, whom he named after his father—Demos, and when young Demos was grown and married, he, too, went into dairy farming. The whole family lived close to the Lord.

One night in 1953, young Demos was home with his wife, and he felt impelled to share with her a thought that had been striking him a great deal lately. He said: "Rose, I have the feeling that there's going to be a Holy Ghost revival in the world and we'll be part of it."

"I know," said Rose. This often happened between them, as though they could read each other's minds, as though they were receiving the same guidance.

Demos said: "I wonder what the Lord wants us to do?"

"He'll let us know," said Rose. "Let's just pray and wait."

They prayed. They waited. Weeks passed.

One night, Demos announced: "I know what the Lord wants me to do."

"So do I," said Rose.

Demos said: "I even know where he wants me to start."

Rose nodded. "He told me, too."

He grinned at her, challenging. "Where?"

"Fresno."

"That's right."

A few days later, Demos Shakarian went into Fresno and visited some businessmen he knew and introduced himself to some others he did not know, and he told them all what the Lord wanted him to do. A few weeks later, in Fresno, the first meeting was held of what became known as the Full Gospel Business Men's Fellowship. Its purpose: to encourage people to become more responsive to the Holy Spirit while remaining active members of their own churches. In less than twenty years, the Fellowship grew into an international organization of more than eight hundred different groups with membership in the hundreds of thousands. So when the young Jesus People came along, they already had more friends than they realized.

—That day when Tony and Susan Alamo took their kids to the Full Gospel meeting at Santa Monica, they were desperately in need of their rent money. They didn't even have to mention money. Somebody passed a hat and raised the precise amount.

—When, late in 1971, the Jesus People in the Midwest were unable to raise the money for a rally or even get a permit for one, the Full Gospel members around Chicago rented the main dining rooms in two of the city's biggest hotels and guaranteed to cover any expenses the Jesus People couldn't meet.

—When, on December 3, 1960, John Sherrill received the Baptism, it was while he was in Atlantic City, attending a convention of the Full Gospel Business Men's Fellowship.

So the leaders of the Jesus Movement were right when they told me that what was happening among the Jesus People really wasn't anything new. It wasn't. And it wasn't fleeting. But what struck me, though, was the way all the pieces kept falling into place.

6

Three Wise Men and a Woman

I kept hearing about the Hollywood Prez. I thought people were referring to the Hollywood *Press,* some newspaper. But, it turned out, they were referring to the Hollywood Presbyterian Church and, in doing so, to Don Williams, its minister to college students. The church complex, occupying a whole block, was just a few minutes from Hollywood and Vine, a hub for hippies, runaways, hustlers and Jesus People around the clock. I was told that drugs changed hands here more often than Bible tracts. The Jesus People at Hollywood Prez drew many of its members from this busy intersection, but the group attracted a lot of students from the colleges that abound in the Los Angeles area, some of them with hang-ups no worse than the generation gap.

Don Williams was in his early thirties when I met him, and he was soon to be married. He was tall and lean and good looking; he wore a suit and he had on a tie. Judging from pictures I had seen of him, he'd recently had a haircut. Williams told me he had been converted at a youth rally while in high school and decided to enter the ministry, Later, he earned his Ph.D. from Union Seminary and Columbia University, and he held a Woodrow Wilson Fellowship at Princeton. When Hollywood Prez was ready for its youth program, Don Williams went home to California. He was probably the best qualified leader in the Jesus Movement that I met.

And yet, for a church-oriented man, his sympathies were definitely with the kids. He said: "We're brought up to feel that we are supposed to look to the Establishment for our values in things like love and peace and truth and hope. Well, if you think there's much love around, check out the rate of breakdowns in families these days. If you want to know about the peace we have, talk to anybody fresh back from Vietnam or just take a look at our national budget for the military next year. Truth? Do a little reading about the mind-games people play. As for hope, it wasn't the people's disappointment that forced Lyndon Johnson out of office; it was the people's despair."

He said: "The Jesus movement exploded out of the cultural tragedy of our day, out of the emptiness of ideals that had no foundations. Young people were idealistic. Most of the Disciples were young: they were attracted by Jesus's ideals: they didn't know who he really was at first, not until he told them. Today's young people are the same. Even those from church-going families really didn't know who Jesus was. Most churches are just social centers, anyway, and any religion that is handed out is Pablum. The kids needed something more. They looked for it in drugs, in sex, in alcohol, in just hitting the road. Some looked for it in student riots and marches. But they didn't find it. They're finding it now, though. They're finding it in Jesus. In the Bible. They are finding something that won't change on them, they won't pull the rug from under them, something that won't turn out to be phony. And that's all they wanted all along."

Because of his understanding the young, one of the first things Williams did at Hollywood Prez, in 1968, was to open the Salt Company Coffeehouse. In this case, the salt referred to being the salt of the earth. And Williams rounded up some rock musicians. He told me:

"If you want to get a bunch of kids together, just let them know there's going to be some music. Music is the language of today's kids. They editorialize in their music. Look at the mob that went to Woodstock. But look at Woodstock. Jesus wasn't there. The kids spent a week getting stoned and smashed and pregnant. I feel that love died at Woodstock for the kids who were there. I doubt that rock could ever pull off another Woodstock. But rock-gospel could. And Jesus would be there."

It's possible that rock-gospel music was born at the Salt Company Coffeehouse. Larry Norman, probably the superstar of rock-gospel, was converted at the coffeehouse and tried out some of his first rock-gospel compositions there. Since then, Norman's records have consistently hit the charts.

Besides the coffeehouse, Don Williams started the Virgil House Christian Communal, two houses, one for girls, one for boys, each able to accommodate fifteen people. Usually the residents are also on the drug rehabilitation program Williams started. Many of them have had the one-minute withdrawal, but most of them are very run-down physically and very unsteady emotionally, and so the communal life proves beneficial as they regain their strengths.

Williams felt that one of the strengths of the Jesus Movement was the fact that the active leadership was comprised of the young themselves. Though there was usually an adult somewhere in the background—like himself—the leadership during services and witnessing and Bible studies was with the young. In an article he wrote for *Christianity Today,* Williams stated:

"What are distinguishing features of the Jesus Movement? First of all, this spiritual outburst is student-led. The initiative has passed from the professional Christian worker, be he pastor, youth worker, or campus-ministry member. Up until now, youth evangelism has been inaugurated by adults. Now it comes by youth. The same hip teen-ager who last year turned his friends on to drugs may now be turning them on to Jesus. In an era when students have led the protests against war and racism, we should not be surprised that they have taken the Gospel of Christ and moved it into their world. Tens of thousands are evangelists today rather than just a few paid professionals.

"Furthermore, this student leadership is emerging out of the youth culture with integrity. We are not being subjected to the embarrassing spectacle of adults who look like flower-children with pot-bellies. We would expect composer Larry Norman to release an album of gospel-rock music because this music is Larry. His conversion has not suddenly given him a taste for Christian tunes in waltz and fox-trot tempo. Lonnie Frisbee, of Calvary Chapel, wears long hair and a beard as he preaches to thousands, because Lonnie was a long-haired 'freak' before his conversion. Becoming a Christian has not meant a crew-cut because that's not Lonnie."

Even so, there was one area where Don Williams wouldn't let the kids run free without proper training, and that was the area of Bible studies. He told me: "Yes, the kids get the Baptism and most of them speak in tongues, but that's not the most important thing. If the Jesus People are going to become lasting Christians, the most important thing is a thorough and correct understanding of the Bible, not just so they can rip off chapter and verse during street debates but so they can apply the Bible properly to their own lives."

For this reason, Hollywood Prez got a new Sunday School, half a black long, and it was being used every night. Bible studies were not looked upon as a college course you could finish, get credit for, and then go out and do likewise. Instead, Bible studies have become a part of life, an endless part of life, with ministers and Bible scholars teaching the teachers who teach the mature Jesus People, who in turn teach the less mature, who in turn teach the newcomers, and the newcomers weren't being turned loose for street-witnessing until they were qualified to do some teaching themselves.

I asked Williams what he, as a minister, felt the Jesus Movement was doing to churches.

"For one thing," he said, "the Movement is removing the labels from churches. The kids don't care which church you go to: if you're a Christian, you're a Christian, and we all ought to be able to worship together. It would be ironic if the ecumenical movement, which is causing so much trouble among the leadership of churches, should be carried out by the kids at the grass roots.

"Another thing that is happening is that the Jesus People know the churches where they're not wanted, so they don't go there. At the same time, however, they are drawing away from those churches their friends who want to worship with them in the way that they worship. Before long, a lot of churches won't have any young people.

"And this. The sacraments are no longer the property of the clergy. It used to be that you had to be baptized by a minister, and it used to be that baptism was a personal and usually a private commitment of your life to Christ. Today anybody can baptize, and today baptism has become a meaningful public act, a witnessing to the world that you have become a Christian, and that you will now work for Christ as well as live for him.

"Another thing. Communion is no longer part of a Sunday morning church service. Communion is what it was supposed to be—a love feast. The Jesus People re-enact the Last Supper in their homes and in their communes every day, and they do it with love. They love one another and show it with an outstretched hand or a meal or a place to crash. The fact that there are hundreds of Christian communes out here is more than a hangover from the hippie world; it is the fulfillment of the quest for 'community' by alienated youth.

"I also think that the Jesus People may be the only way we are going to be able to preserve marriage as a social institution as well as a spiritual one. Most of these kids come from homes where the marriage turned into a disaster. They've seen divorces, they're seen separations, they've seen infidelity. They figured that a marriage ceremony was just a license to have intercourse, so why bother with the license? But then they become Christians and they study their Bibles and their attitudes change. They find out that they're not supposed to fornicate or commit adultery. In Ephesians, they see where Paul compares marriage to the relationship between Christ and the church, and they learn that this is the way a Christian marriage should be. They know now that Christ's presence in a marriage provides grace that brings the two people closer together and assures peace and loyalty in a home. Yes, the kids just might do it."

Whether the kids achieve this within the church or on the outside of it doesn't make any difference to the kids, Williams told me. "The kids know where they stand," he said. "Now it's up to the churches to move." In his magazine article, he said:

"Adult Christianity in America is too often uptight and performance-oriented. We preach justification by faith and live justification by works. Our worship tends to be cold and impersonal. We are guilty of judging by appearance, as did the Pharisees. Now a new stream of the Spirit is moving across the land. Tens of thousands of youths are 'turning on' to Jesus. They need to find the full body of Christ. They need to know of Christ's Lordship over all of life. They need grounding in the Word of God. Their gifts to us are zeal, and love in true community. Can we receive from them and give to them? This decade of church history will be determined not by the success or failure of the NCC (National Council of Churches) and COCU (Conference On Christian Unity) but by our response to the Jesus Movement."

The place was beautiful. It had once been a resort hotel for movie stars and business leaders. The atmosphere was heavy with elegance and wealth. Now it was the world headquarters for Campus Crusade For Christ, founded in 1951 by Bill Bright, a successful Los Angeles businessman. Bright's office was on the second floor of the six-story building. His secretary had to unlock his hallway door with a key to let me in. The office was oval and spacious, a symphony of blues and whites. So was Bill Bright, who has to hold first prize as the best-dressed man in the Jesus Movement. Off to one side was a small desk; in the center of the room was a round coffee table, with three or four chairs, and it was here that Bill Bright received his visitors. A few papers were neatly off to one side. My first impression was: This is an organized man. He turned out to be precisely that.

Bill Bright was born in Oklahoma. On finishing school, he went to Los Angeles and entered business with Bright's California Confections—a fancy food line. He had always been a devout Christian, and so it was not surprising to his friends that, in 1946, he decided to study for the ministry. By then he was engaged to Vonette, a girl from home, who was finishing college in Texas. Bright entered the Princeton Theological Seminary, meanwhile continuing to run his business by long-distance telephone. A year of this proved to be too demanding, his studies and business interfering with each other. He therefore transferred to the Fuller Theological Seminary back in California. He also got married.

From the start, the Brights agreed that the Lord would come first in their lives. More as a lark than anything else, they one day went into separate rooms and made a list of what each wanted most for their marriage, and the two lists were almost alike. They both wanted to live holy lives, controlled and empowered by the Holy Spirit; they wanted to be fruitful in their witness for Christ; they wanted to help fulfill the Great Commission in their generation, the commission being the total evangelization of the world. Now it was a lark no longer. Both signed their lists as a contract with God.

Gradually Bill phased himself out of his business; Vonette took a job teaching. They led busy church lives. Bill taught a Bible class of under- and post-graduate students. Together the Brights ministered in jails and hospitals and Skid Row missions. They began to notice that they had to wait to get into the jails and hospitals and missions—so many other church groups were trying to get at the same people. The Brights noticed, too, that the path to the college students and especially to business executives was practically clear. Bill wondered why these present and future leaders of the community were being neglected.

One night in 1951, in his last semester at Fuller, Bill and a classmate were at the Brights' home in Hollywood studying for final exams. It was very late; Vonette had already gone to bed. Then, as Bill later put it: "Suddenly, without warning or without any indication of what was going to happen, I sensed the presence of God in a way I had never known before. . . . Though it could not have lasted more than a few seconds, I suddenly had the overwhelming impression that the Lord had unfolded a scroll of instructions of what I was to do with my life."

Bill looked across the desk at his friend. He said: "Hugh, the Lord just told me what he wants me to do with my life."

Hugh did not look up. "Really?"

"Yes. It's true. Hugh, I have felt God's presence in this room. He told me—He showed me—what kind of work He wants me to do."

Hugh looked up. "What kind?"

"He wants me to work with college students."

"You're going to become a college chaplain?"

"No. I'm not going to be ordained. The Lord wants me to carry out this ministry as a layman."

"You're not going to be ordained?"

"No."

"Hey, you're not just trying to dodge the exams, are you?"

"Of course not. I'll take the exams. I want my degree. But I'm not going to be ordained."

Hugh glanced at his watch. It was very late. "Okay," he said, and went back to his papers.

After Hugh left, Bill awoke Vonette and told her what had happened. She understood. She believed. Together they praised God and promised to obey Him.

Next morning at school, Bill Bright shared his experience with Dr. Wilbur Smith, his English Bible professor, a man widely known in the church as a scholar and author. Smith got excited. He kept saying: "This is of God. This is of God." He offered to help in any way he could; he promised to pray. And the next day, as Bill entered the classroom, Dr. Smith handed him a piece of paper on which was written: "CCC."

Bill asked: "What does it mean?"

Smith said: "Campus Crusade For Christ. That's what you're starting."

Bill nodded. "Yes, I guess it is."

"It came to me during my prayers last night."

"Then that's what we'll call it."

Being an organized man, Bill Bright's first efforts for Campus Crusade was to form an organization. He had no specific idea of what kind of work he would actually do or even how he would get started, but he knew that he would need the advice and prayers of older and more experienced men. So he went to friends he had come to know through the church, through his studies, and in business, and he invited them to join his board of directors. Among those who accepted were Dr. Smith and Billy Graham.

But where to begin? And how to begin? One thing was clear: if the Brights intended to *get* to the students they had to be *near* the students, which meant that they would have to move. Also, it occurred to the Brights that the students at the University of California at Los Angeles could do with some information about Jesus Christ—they were already certainly getting enough information about Karl Marx. Checking on houses in the area, the Brights found that the rents were outrageous. But they knew they had to be near the campus. One realtor had a picture of a house that seemed perfect, both in its self and in its location, a block from sorority row, but the rent on it was $450, more than twice the Brights could afford. But then Bill learned that the house was owned by two sisters who wanted to leave in a week for a year's tour of South America, and they were getting desperate for a tenant. Bill went to see them and told them why he wanted the house, but that he could pay only $200 a month. The sisters said they would let him know. Before he reached home, the sisters had called Vonette and said the Brights could have the house for $200, provided they would add $25 a month for the gardener. It was a deal.

Thus the headquarters for Campus Crusade For Christ found its first home. Over the next ten years, the headquarters moved to another house in Los Angeles and to an estate in Minnesota before acquiring the hotel at Arrowhead Springs in 1962. Bill Bright told me: "Each time, the Lord provided others to take the financial burden off our shoulders." With the second Los Angeles house, it was a rich woman. The house was a veritable castle, with reception rooms big enough to hold the crowds that were now coming to nightly meetings, but the price was fit for a king.

Bill Bright happened to mention the house to the rich woman, who was a friend, and she said: "Is that place available? I've had my eyes on it for years. I'll buy it but I don't want to live in it alone. You and Vonette come and live with me. All you have to do is cover your own expenses, and you can use as much of the place as you need for your work." And the Minnesota property was a gift, through Bill Greig, chairman of the Midwest Keswick, whose group didn't need the land anymore but wanted it to go to some organization that would use it to glorify God.

The acquisition of the hotel was slightly less than miraculous. Bright had never seen the hotel until he learned that it was for sale, and when he saw it he knew that he was going to get it for Campus Crusade. This was not merely determination. The same presence of God which Bright had felt that night he was studying for his finals was felt again, and it was from this that Bill Bright took his confidence. He left everything to the Lord. The price of the hotel and about eighteen hundred acres of land was two million dollars. The owners were ready to sell to Bright on a deposit of $15,000 and a first payment of $130,000 within a month. On sheer faith, Bright borrowed the deposit from a bank and then got on the phone to his friends in business for the first payment. The deal was closed at the end of 1962, and Bright was faced with what looked like centuries of heavy monthly payments. A few months later, however, a wealthy construction engineer said that he would give Bright $300,000 if Bright could raise the balance of the debt in a year. At the time, the debt was better than $1.5 million. Checking with the former owners, Bright was told that if he could, in fact, pay the debt in a year they would drop $100,000 of the balance, and there would be a savings of $120,000 in interest. In all, then, $520,000 was involved, leaving Bright with about a million to raise. Again on sheer faith, he took the challenge. He made it clear, however, that he was not about to become a full-time fund-raiser—his ministry to the students came first.

It was nip and tuck right down to the finish line. On the last day of the agreement, Bright was still $33,000 short. Just as the family was getting ready for bed at ten, Bright found a note in his pocket, a message from his secretary: a friend from Denver had called and wanted Bright to call back. Bright had forgotten. At first, Bright thought it might be too late to call—eleven in Denver, but then he decided to make the call. The friend said he had $5,000 to contribute to the fund if it was needed. Bright said that it sure was. So they were down to $28,000.

The Denver call reminded Bill Bright that an Arizona businessman had given Campus Crusade some property in Colorado for which a Denver lawyer had once offered $17,000. Despite the hour, Bright called the lawyer and asked for $22,000. He got $18,000. So they were down to $10,000. They had less than an hour to go. Just then, Bright's business manager knocked on the door, and the man had tears in his eyes. Staff members who lived on the grounds had gathered in the lobby for prayers. Spontaneously, they had taken up a collection among themselves and given it to the business manager. It was only a few hundred dollars, but it was like a million. And there was something else.

Months before, a donation of $5,000 had been made to the general operating fund, and it had not been touched. The business manager felt it would be all right to transfer the money to the hotel fund. He said: "That would leave five thousand. Do you think you can raise it?"

"There's only one place," Bright said. He picked up his telephone and asked the operator to find Congressman Walter Judd of Minnesota, no matter where the man was. Judd, a former medical missionary, had attended meetings at headquarters and, learning about the fund drive, had offered five thousand dollars if the drive fell short. Judd was located at his home. Bill Bright reminded him of the offer, then asked: "Can you spare it?"

Judd asked: "How soon do you need it?"

Bright glanced at the wall clock. "In about thirty seconds."

Judd said: "You've got it. I'll mail the check in the morning."

That did it.

The place is beautiful, and the beauty can be deceptive. You keep looking around for the Cadillacs that should go with a place like this. There are no Cadillacs. Bill Bright doesn't even own a car at all. When he needs a car, a friend who is a dealer loans him one. Bright must also have a friend who owns a haberdashery; Bright can't afford to dress that well on his salary. At Campus Crusade, the starting salary for unmarrieds is $285 a month, with $10 per month raises over five years to the top of $335. For marrieds, the starting salary is $425 a month, with monthly increments of $20 over five years to a top of $525. A monthly allowance of $30 is made for up to four children, with gradual raises up to $100 a month as the kids enter college. Bill Bright, who has two sons, isn't being paid as much as some of his assistants who have more kids. So nobody goes to work for Campus Crusade for the money. In fact, a number of business executives and professional people have left well-paying jobs or private practice in order to work with the Crusade. Furthermore, staff members are expected to raise as much of their salary as they can. Some do this by one-man fund-raising wherever they are stationed. Others get on the payroll of a church or some organization that is related to student work, the Crusade making up the difference between what they earn and what is set for them by headquarters. I make a point out of this because anybody who visits the luxurious headquarters and sees Bill Bright in his luxurious clothes is liable to get a different impression.

At first, Campus Crusade For Christ was a one-man show—Bill, with a one-woman staff—Vonette. Bill continued to work as he had before. He would telephone a sorority or fraternity house and invite himself over as an after-dinner speaker, and any students who were interested in listening to him would remain in the dining hall after the meal. In all the times Bright had done this, not once did a student come up to him afterward and say that he—or she—wanted to know more about Jesus Christ, perhaps even make a commitment to him. But after the vision, after the Campus Crusade For Christ came into being, the Holy Spirit seemed to be using Bright more effectively. Crowds started going up to him; crowds started showing up for meetings at his home.

Bill Bright sensed that the Lord did not expect him to limit the Crusade to UCLA; and he realized that if the movement was to spread, it would need a trained leadership. And he would have to do the training. Once again, he went to his friends, friends in the church, friends from the seminary, friends in business, and from these areas of his life Bill Bright acquired his first staff. In a year, Campus Crusade For Christ was at work at San Diego State, University of Southern California, at Berkeley, Oregon State and Washington University.

When the Crusade headquarters moved into the Arrowhead hotel in 1963, Bill had a staff of about 125. At the beginning of 1972, he had a staff of over a thousand, about two-thirds of them out in the field. And Bill Bright had big plans.

Oversimplified, the principle of Campus Crusade For Christ is that if you will turn over your life completely to Jesus Christ he will provide you, through the Holy Spirit, with the guidance to solve your problems. This doesn't mean that you will never have any problems, nor does it mean that you will never sweat over the problems you have; but it can mean that your complete trust in Jesus Christ will make you more sensitive to his guidance, and you will know what to do. Of course, more will be required of you than turning your life over to Jesus. You will have to live a Christian life yourself. Prayer. The Bible. Church. Witnessing. Christian conduct in your relations with others. Even all this will not help you raise a million dollars in a year, unless, like Bill Bright, you want it not for yourself but for the glory of God, and God knows when you are getting tricky.

Based on material in Paul's Epistles, Bill Bright speaks in terms of three kinds of people: 1) the "natural" man, who doesn't believe in Jesus Christ, who runs his life for his own self-interests, and whose life is usually one of discord and frustration; 2) the "carnal" man, who believes in Jesus but who relies upon his own efforts to get through life, usually fouling himself up; and 3) the "spiritual" man, whose life is Christ controlled and Holy Spirit empowered, resulting in harmony with God's plan, a plan that could only be for your spiritual fulfillment. Bright has said:

"We have discovered that when we truly train people, they are inspired to a height of dedication that one cannot possibly experience through inspiration alone. It is my strong conviction that true inspiration is the result of a very strong training program. From the very inception of this ministry our major thrusts have been: first, aggressive evangelism; then, training men; then, building disciples and sending them forth for Christ. Even in a conference in which a number of non-Christians are present, if the majority of those present are Christians, almost all of our messages are designed to build the Christian in the faith and challenge him to become a disciple. We train carnal Christians to become spiritual Christians, teaching them the difference between walking in the flesh and walking in the Spirit, and showing them how to share their faith in Christ more effectively with others. The end result is that within a matter of a few hours after the carnal Christians have become spiritual Christians and have learned how to communicate their faith, they begin to share Christ with the non-believers at the conference or institute. Thus, more people come to Christ through the awakened Christians than we could ever hope to reach for Christ through directing all of our messages toward non-Christians. Of course, the Christians are also greatly benefited through their experience of introducing others to Christ."

On the basis of this sort of training and development, Bill Bright has made some staggering projections for Campus Crusade For Christ. His entire organization is geared to the effort of having a staff of 10,000 by 1975. As a result of their growing influence, Bright feels that there will also exist by 1975 what he calls the Great Commission Army, by then with a membership of five million. These people would be what Bright now calls disciples, people who have become Spiritual Christians through their contact with the Campus Crusade, perhaps in school or in the military or in business. They would be apart from Campus Crusade, with their own leadership, and with their allegiance to their own churches, since they would be of all Christian denominations. In 1975, then, these five million volunteers would start moving out, armed with the Gospel, to witness to carnal Christians and to non-believers. Bill Bright believes that their number should be increased to an army of fifty million Spiritual Christians in a year. Then the fifty million will move out, witnessing. At this rate, Bright feels, every human being living on this planet will have had an encounter with a Spiritual Christian, a discussion with him, and a chance to make his own decision to commit his life to Jesus Christ by the year 1980.

Hal Lindsey, who perhaps can be called the Apostle of the End Times, is on the staff of Campus Crusade For Christ. Lindsey purports that the generation which will enter its maturity—the forties—at the time of the Second Coming of Jesus Christ was born in the few years after the creation of Israel in 1948. This would put us around 1990, give or take a few years. It would also mean that the last war will have been going on a few years.

At Arrowhead Springs, the computer data-processing machines that will be necessary to handle the paperwork for the Great Commission Army have already been installed.

Jack Sparks said: "I am a lapsed professor."

He looked more like a businessman who had just come in from a hunting trip and wanted to get some paperwork done before going upstairs to dress for dinner. We were in his basement office in one of the dozen communes he runs in the San Francisco area, this one in Berkeley, a few minutes from the university campus. The room was monastically plain. There was no rug on the concrete floor. The walls were bulletin boards of printed material in various stages of publication. Sparks' desk was small, old and littered. A man of medium height and build, Sparks' dark hair was receding but worn full at the back; he had an overgrown Van Dyke. From his clothes, he could, indeed, have just returned from hunting; he could also have just come off a construction job. The intelligence in his face indicated that, whatever he did, he would have been the boss. He was in his early forties, married, and with a teen-aged son who is an excellent photographer. Sparks considered himself a lifelong Spiritual Christian, although he did not use that expression.

Sparks was educated in a westerly direction, receiving his bachelor's degree at the University of Pennsylvania, his master's at Purdue, and his doctorate, in psychological statistics, at Iowa. He became a professor of behavioral psychology at Colorado. During the school year of 1967-68, Sparks grew increasingly aware of the soaring drug scene on campus. As a psychologist, he knew there had to be more reasons for it than the peer-group pressures to which so many addicts attributed their habit. From discussion and studies, he observed that there was a lacing of negative influences in the life of each addict, and the one thread that appeared in each case was a weak spiritual foundation.

Sparks already knew the fieldman for Campus Crusade For Christ at Colorado, and he talked to him about this. Sparks also talked to his wife about it. The two of them talked about it with three couples they knew. Then all eight of them headed for Arrowhead Springs for training.

Jack Sparks wanted to work in Berkeley, where the campus was a hotbed of radicals who were attracting thousands of young idealists and warping them into non-believers in God and in this country. This was a departure for Campus Crusade, but Bill Bright offered to back Sparks until he was on his own feet financially. Sparks headed north in April, 1969. Housing was too expensive in Berkeley, so Sparks found a place in Oakland, but every night he was on Telegraph Avenue, a street lined with coffeeshops, bars and bookstores, and he was rapping with the students. Sparks started what he called the Christian World Liberation Front, its name pointedly political to stir student curiosity, but its goal was individual liberation by Christianity from all the hang-ups that were bugging the kids.

Of all the Jesus People groups I met, Sparks' was the only one that took on public issues—the war, Pakistan, pollution, unemployment, civil rights, overpopulation, corruption, the whole scene. Surprisingly, the CWLF was usually on the same side with the radicals in terms of criticizing the Establishment, but the big difference was in the approach to the solutions. The Front said: "You can't change the System by destroying it. You've got to change people." *Right On!,* Sparks' bi-weekly tabloid, was the only Jesus People newspaper I saw that carried articles and comments on topical events, although the editorial tone was, understandably, Christ-centered.

From the start, Jack Sparks was taking kids home with him for the night. He had managed to conquer the hippie lingo quickly, and the kids were surprised to find (in their eyes) an old man who not only spoke their language but also shared their concerns for the world and, like them, wanted to do something about it. As I found out, Sparks encourages Front members to be active in campus affairs; several of them have been elected to the student governing body. They are always ready to picket City Hall.

As soon as Sparks' newspaper, pamphlets and books began to bring in money, he started acquiring houses in Berkeley, usually by renting them. In a little more than two years, he opened six houses in town and two ranch-communes out in the country. They were not, Sparks made it clear, crash pads, although the doors were always open to anybody who needed a meal or a place to rest. Also, the ranches and the houses were self-supporting. Whether a resident was a student or not, he was expected to put up between fifty and seventy-five dollars a week to keep the place running. Each place was under the supervision of an elder who was also the spiritual head of the household, leading group worship and Bible studies.

I attended one of Sparks' Bible classes one evening. It was held in the large living room in the house on Dwight Way, where Sparks had his office in the basement. About fifty people were there, mostly kids, and they all had Bibles. Some of them also had notebooks and took notes during the discussion. We started out with the singing, to the accompaniment of a guitar. Then the discussion began. I expected Jack Sparks to do most of the talking, the teaching, but instead he comported himself more like a catalyst, throwing out questions, igniting little debates by asking this boy whether what that girl had said was a correct interpretation, bringing out the shy ones, guiding the conversation away from the two or three who tried to hog it, making little jokes when the atmosphere got a bit tense, telling everyone to pause and meditate a moment when the dialogue got too confused. He was still the professor, opening up young minds.

Before the meeting ended, a hat was passed. Jack Sparks said: "If you've got any money to spare, put it in. If you need some, take it out." About fifteen people put something in; five or six took something out. As far as I could see, I was the only person who put in any folding money. I passed the hat to the young man on my left, who dropped in a couple of coins, and then he passed it to his left, to a small Spanish boy with a massive umbrella of black kinky hair. The guy took out my two bucks. I didn't mind that so much, but I had seen the kid around the place all day, I knew he was a resident, and I thought he should have wanted the money to go to the house. Then I caught myself and rejected the thought, remembering that the theme of the Bible discussion had been that we shouldn't judge each other, lest we be judged.

One of Sparks' most unique contributions to the Jesus People literature is a translation of Paul's Epistles into the hippie vernacular, which is what most Jesus People speak. I noticed that King James was the version used mostly by the Jesus People, and King James, with its Sixteenth-Century English, can be difficult to comprehend even if you've got the Baptism. With Sparks' permission, here is how he translated First Corinthians, Chapters 15 and 16. The idea being discussed is the universal resurrection of the faithful upon the Second Coming, and the excerpt starts around Chapter 15, Verse 30.

"If these things aren't true, why should we place ourselves in front of people who hate us? Why should brothers and sisters in repressive societies be giving up their lives for Jesus? Dig it! Why should we, in our lives with Jesus, die daily to self? Yep, if the dead don't rise, let's get stoned and forget it.

"Don't let people who talk like that fool you. They'll drag you down on their trips if they can. Get straight and stop messing with God. Man, some of these people don't know God at all and it's a shame for you to listen to them.

"Now somebody's going to come down on you and ask, 'If people come back from the dead, how's it gonna happen and what are they gonna look like?' OK, jiver, why don't you *think* once? Plant some seeds. What comes up? The same seeds you planted? Of course not, fool! They have to die and what comes up is something different. You put a dried-up little seed in the ground and God brings something green up—apple trees from apple seeds, rose bushes from rose seeds, etc. People and birds and fish and animals have different kinds of bodies. Also, angels have different bodies than people and each is beautiful in its own way. And the sun and the moon and the stars are all different and each of them is beautiful in its own way too. So dig it! Our bodies which are going to die and rot are different from the ones we'll have when we come back to life again. Those bodies will never die. So the bodies we have now will be 'planted' in death only to be raised to new life;

'planted' in weakness and raised to new life in God's power. At the time of death they are just lifeless human bodies, but when they come back to life they will be supernatural forever bodies—the second exists just as surely as does the first. Just as the first man, Adam, was given a living human body, the last Adam, Jesus, brought the life-giving spirit. So, we've got our human bodies and someday God will give us new supernatural bodies. God made Adam's body out of natural elements just like what the earth's made of. But He remade Jesus' body in heaven. We're all made of the same stuff Adam was, but those of us who know Jesus will be remade with a body just like His. Our bodies now reflect the earth, but someday our bodies will reflect heaven.

"Dig it, sisters and brothers, these flesh and blood bodies can't be part of God's forever nation—they aren't built to last. But here's a secret that you can't forget: we won't all die but we all will have new bodies. And when we have those brand-new bodies, the Old Testament prophecy will finally be true for us all just like it was for Jesus. 'Death is swallowed up in victory! O death, where is your sting? Where is your victory!' Death's barb is slavery to wrong and its powerful constant reminder is the law. But thank You, Jesus, You gave us the victory! So, brothers and sisters, stand! Be strong; don't get messed over; work hard for Jesus 'cause nothing you do for Him will be wasted.

"P. S. Don't forget to share your bread with the brothers and sisters who need it. A good way to do it is to save what you don't need yourself and give it to them when something comes up.

"Keep your eyes open. Keep the faith. Don't get caught in people's trips. Be strong and do everything in love.

"Maranatha! Right on! Jesus' love be with you all."

Jack Sparks was one of the busiest leaders of the Movement I met, his secretary at his side as the two of them continued to work at other things as we talked. Even so, he should take time some day to sit down to Genesis and make the trip all the way through.

People kept telling me to wait until I met Linda Meissner—what a woman. Then, just a few days before I did meet her, attitudes changed. A great tragedy had befallen Linda, people said. She had merged with the Children of God. Ordinarily, the Jesus People were extremely charitable, and I did not hear one leader criticize another. A few of them told me: "For me, this is not an ego trip. I am not on an ego trip." Implying, I assumed, that some of the others may have been. But the Children of God was the only Jesus People group of which I did not hear one good word. They were even accused of being "of the devil." And now the great Linda Meissner had joined up with them. People were sad and disappointed and worried. I was told that I would probably not be allowed to see Linda now, and that if I did get to see her I would not be left alone with her. At least two others would be present.

Well, I did get to see Linda Meissner. The only trouble I had was in locating her. The two Seattle numbers I had were disconnected. The Children of God had taken a new headquarters, the building of a social organization—the German-American Association or something like that—and nobody knew the phone number. So I just kept telephoning likely leads until I located the Children. Linda was not there, but she was due around ten. I was there at ten. At five after ten, I was with Linda.

We were not alone. We were in a large office. About twenty feet away in one direction was a girl at a typewriter; about twenty feet in another direction was a boy at a drawing board. Sitting with us was a young man who said his name was Jethro. I knew that wasn't his real name. On joining the Children of God, you discard your former identity and take a new name from the Bible. Jethro was in charge. Definitely.

Linda Meissner was a small, slender girl, pretty, with long, brown hair and deeply-set eyes. Her coloring was a natural beige, and I couldn't tell whether she was wearing make-up. She had on a two-piece grey suit and high heels. I already knew she had married recently, to a Seattle policeman who had five children by a former marriage, but Linda was not wearing a wedding ring. One word described her: tenseness. Throughout our three-hour visit, her hands were clasped tightly in her lap most of the time. She spoke softly, quickly. Jethro did most of the talking, and when he and I would go off on some tangent, I could hear Linda, on my left, exclaiming softly "Praise Jesus" and "Praise the Lord" and "Oh, my sweet Jesus" and "Right on!"

Linda Meissner was born on a farm in Iowa, and she went to a Bible college in Missouri. She began her work for the Lord as a member of a trio that sang at revivals and gave witness. In 1961, Linda went to work for Dave Wilkerson who had just opened his first Teen Challenge Center in Brooklyn. It was a rough job. Linda's main effort was to break through to the Debs, the distaff side of the Brooklyn gangs. One night after services, Linda and a partner, Kay Ware, went out to make contact with some girls. Passing a sandwich shop, they saw four girls in a booth over Cokes and went in and joined them. Within minutes, Linda was talking about Jesus to the girls, and the girls were listening intently. Some boys wandered over, and one of the girls told them to go away. But they hovered nearby and they heard what Linda was saying and they got angry. They began to taunt her with sexy invitations. Linda looked up at one boy and said: "God bless you." Stunned at first, the boy came on even stronger. Finally, Linda and Kay invited the four girls to attend services at the center the next evening, and they left. Several boys followed them, taunting, making passes. Then, for no apparent reason, one of the boys suggested that they all forget these two chicks, and the girls went on alone. That night, as Linda wrote home, she said: "You can actually feel the presence of evil here. I know that my life is in danger. I only have one desire—to burn out for God."

After Linda left Brooklyn, she began her career as a preacher, speaking at small revivals across the country. She went to Mexico. She told me: "I was doing very well for the Lord in Mexico. The Lord was really using me. I was bringing a lot of people to the Lord. But then God and I had an argument. He wanted me to come up here to Seattle, but I wanted to stay in Mexico. I was doing so well there. But then God told me that I should remember that I was His child and I had to obey Him. I knew He was right, of course, so I came up here."

She began with street witnessing. Soon a small following developed around her. They met in a private home for prayers and discussion. The following grew. More homes were needed. Then Linda opened a large coffeehouse which she called the Catacombs, and it was packed every night. She held outdoor rallies, at first attracting hundreds, then thousands. She formed the Jesus People Army, that once had a membership of five thousand. She branched out. Her following in Vancouver was almost as great as in Seattle. Down the coast, leaders of the Movement began to hear about Linda, and they went to Seattle to meet her. All of them were impressed by her spirituality, her dedication, the strength of her presence. They invited her to California to preach, and the news that Linda Meissner was going to be at a rally could double a crowd.

Then Linda Meissner joined the Children of God.

The Jesus People went into shock.

I asked Linda why she did it. She said: "I was losing my people. I didn't have any follow-up. I didn't have any organization. The Lord was using me to bring souls to him, but all of a sudden things got so big that they went out of control and I started losing my people. They started drifting back to their old ways."

Another great catch by the Children of God at about the same time was David Hoyt, leader of the Jesus People in Atlanta. Hoyt was working in Vancouver and I did not meet him. *Time,* of January 24, 1972, said of Linda and Hoyt: "Both apparently decided that their own methods were not producing lasting converts; Hoyt pointedly blamed his 'watered-down Gospel.' When he entered the Children of God, he took many of the Atlanta Jesus People with him. Linda Meissner, however, took far fewer of her Jesus People Army along—and indeed the feud between the mainstream Army (including Linda's husband John Salvesen) and her splinter group has scandalized Seattle's Jesus People."

The only awkward moment in my talk with Linda Meissner occurred when, glancing at her ringless hands, I asked: "Are you married?"

She looked at Jethro. Jethro said: "Yes, she is."

I asked: "Is her husband with the Children of God?"

Jethro said: "No. Not yet. But we expect he will be."

The criticisms of the Jesus People about the Children of God were many and varied. The Children of God, I was told, felt that theirs was the only bonafide Jesus movement, that everybody else was in the wrong, and that anybody who wouldn't join them was damned. The Children didn't preach the love of God; they preached the wrath of God. They were supposed to have battle cries proclaiming doom for everybody but themselves. They required their recruits to drop out of society—quit school, quit their jobs, break off from their family and friends. Recruits were also required to turn over all their possessions to the organization. I was told that some of the recruits had actually been shanghaied and others were being held against their will. Some of them were supposed to be subdued by drugs and hypnotism. Mail, incoming and outgoing, was censored. And the Children's policy of discarding their real identity and taking on a Bible name was, people said, providing a haven for draft dodgers, deserters, runaways (both kids and adults) and fugitives from justice.

I brought all this up. Jethro dismissed the bondage complaints as nonsense. For the rest, he had a Bible reference for every point. I noticed, later, when I studied my notes on this interview, that they contained more Bible citations than any other interview I had on the whole trip, more than most of them put together. I checked out the references. Jesus did say that a lot of people would have to break off with their families for his sake. Luke did say that the first Christians held all possessions in common. As for the name changing, I knew that Catholic priests, nuns and lay brothers had been doing that for centuries, not to hide anything but to choose a saint or Bible character whom they wished to emulate. It seemed to me that the fastest way to break up the Children of God would be for the authorities to find out that they were harboring fugitives of any kind; and if the leadership didn't know that, then they were stupid. The mail censorship didn't bother me. I had willingly submitted to that myself both as a Catholic seminarian and a U. S. soldier, and both times I felt this invasion of my privacy was justified, first as a means of more understanding of me and then for the defense of my country. I couldn't go along with the idea that the only way to heaven was the Children's way, and yet I couldn't deny that my own church had promulgated this same idea about itself for a long time. This was probably what bothered me about the Children of God. Their presumption. Their spiritual pride.

Another troubling aspect about the Children is their elusiveness on personal matters and even the organization itself. It was either in 1967 or '68 that David Berg, an itinerant Fundamentalist minister, founded a group called Teens For Christ. In the organization with him were his four children and their husbands and wives. The group first became known for disrupting church services by demonstrations and telling the people they were going to hell. Berg had formerly worked for J. Fred Jordan, a Los Angeles radio and television evangelist. Jordan let Berg's group, by then the Children of God, use as headquarters and commune a ranch he owned in Texas and, as a training center for recruits—"babes"—, a warehouse he owned in a slum section of Los Angeles. The kids started appearing on Jordan's TV show, witnessing, just before Jordan made his pitch for donations to support the project. Berg, who took the name Moses, lived in Texas, from where he occasionally sent out newsletters—"Mo-Letters"—to the Children as they began to spread out across the country, but I was told that the real power in the organizations were Berg's two daughters. In the summer of 1971, Berg and Jordan had a dispute, reportedly over property ownership, and Jordan evicted the Children of God from both the ranch and the warehouse. One group, led by Jethro, headed northward to Seattle. And Linda Meissner.

In a letter from Linda to her followers, dated only "September, 1971," the return address began:

Linda Meissner
Jesus People Army
CHILDREN OF GOD

substantiating the merger rather than indicating a surrender. In the letter, Linda said that she first thought of the merger as she was visiting the Los Angeles colony and saw the vast exhibition of love among the Children. A Movement leader I met later said he had been at a conference of Jesus People leaders in Seattle a week before the news broke about Linda; Linda was at the meeting but the Children of God were not represented, and Linda had not said a word about any merger. In her letter, Linda said she had been greatly impressed by the solid training the Children were giving recruits and that she realized she had been making a mistake by not being as firm with her own. She acknowledged that the weakening of her army was God's punishment for her mistake, and she accepted it as a gift of love. She said:

"In facing our shortcomings and many mistakes of the past, we have been led to have a thorough program of teaching all our visitors who are hungry for the truth, so that the ones who finally end up living with us really want to serve God 100%. We have found that we had appointed a number of young elders who should not have been in positions of leadership and authority, and only became puffed up, and unteachable, so this has now been totally changed . . . 1 Timothy 3:6*. Also, a number of people who have left us, who were only living with us for the loaves and fishes, free rent, and a comfortable place to sleep at night. Thank God that he has helped us to face the transition! We now have six hours of Bible study and thorough training for all our young followers! It's more of a Revolution for Jesus than ever before!!! And now I see that the vision is finally becoming a reality, as Jesus Christ is raising up that rare quality of first-century loyalty, obedience, boldness, and God's love."

She signed the letter "Love." I couldn't decide whether

* "He must not be a convert newly baptized, for fear the sin of conceit should bring him a judgement contrived by the devil."

mailing the letter required a great deal of nerve or a great deal of humility.

Jethro told me that there were about two thousand members in the Children of God in forty colonies across the country. And there had been a recent surge of activity, with a hundred new recruits coming in every week and one new colony starting every week. About fifteen percent of the recruits drop out in the first weeks of training; and of those who persevere through the two-month course, all stay on as disciples. During training, Jethro said, a recruit spent two hours a day at chores, six hours at Bible study, four hours at street-witnessing. In a colony, more time was given to chores, maintaining the place, and this was the only kind of work the Children did.

A recruit was supposed to be of legal age, but I saw several in Seattle who certainly weren't twenty-one and a few who couldn't have been eighteen as yet. And this was another trouble spot for the Children. No matter how badly a boy or girl may want to join the Children of God, they cannot do so legally without their parents' consent. When the consent was not forthcoming, the kids just took off. Efforts by parents to get the children back were fruitless because the kids soon disappeared into the network of colonies in this country and abroad. Out of this problem, the Parents' Committee to Free Our Children from the Children of God was formed in California, with other chapters popping up elsewhere. On the grounds of some of the things these parents have said publicly, the Children of God filed a 1.1 million dollar libel and slander suit against the committee. Also, a Texas mother who reportedly kept her 18-year-old daughter out of the Children of God by having her committed to a mental institution was sued for $300,000. Both Jesus and Paul advised Christians on how to solve their differences, and legal action was to be the last resort, so I didn't care much for this development, either.

I asked Jethro how he had come to join the Children of God. He said he had become a Christian at eighteen, although he turned out to be only a carnal Christian. He got to like money and to like things and he stopped sacrificing.

He went into business on his own as a consultant to companies which were having trouble with their data-processing machines, and he was doing very well.

He said: "But then Jesus spoke to me one night, and I realized how far I had drifted from what he wanted me to be. I quit my job. I paid my bills. I sold everything I owned and I gave the money to the Children of God when I joined up. While I was in training, I met the girl I eventually married. She's here working with us now."

Later in the visit, Jethro threw at me: "Why don't *you* join us?"

I laughed, and I asked: "What would you want with an old man like me?"

"I don't care how old you are," he said. "We've got older people with us. But we're growing very fast, and we're going to put out a lot of publications. We'll need a writer. We'll need an editor. You could do those things for us."

I said: "Let me pay my bills. Then I'll think about it."

I knew I would never do it. I have a lot of complaints about the Catholic Church, but I have no intention of walking out of it as yet. Besides, as I had already found out, I could become an active Jesus Person and stay where I was. But, as we talked on, I looked at Linda, and I wondered what I would have done had she been the one to put the challenge to me. It would have been difficult to dodge with her. She was, it seemed to me, completely sincere and dedicated, with a consuming love for souls.

She said: "Do you realize that eighty people die in every second of the day? Eighty people suddenly find themselves standing before God, waiting for Him to judge their souls? Many of them aren't ready to be judged. We have no time to waste. We must get well-trained disciples as soon as we can. We must save souls."

As I was leaving, I was impelled to kiss Linda on her forehead. She smiled for the first time in three hours.

Later, in another city, I was discussing Linda Meissner with another leader of the Jesus People, and I reported the great concern for friends in the Movement felt for her. The young man said: "Oh, don't worry about Linda. Linda is a very strong woman. I know that the two Berg sisters are supposed to be running the Children of God; but if I know Linda at all, she can take over the whole outfit whenever she decides that she should."

If she ever does, I hope she won't need any writers.

7

One In The Spirit

From the first day, I met Jesus People who had been Catholics and Jews. Some of the leaders pointed this out to me as evidence of ecumenism; but then I learned that these particular individuals had not really been practicing their faith for some time, and, although I was glad they were back at their prayers, I could not regard them as pioneers in the repairs to Christianity. I knew there were Catholic

Jesus People within the Catholic Church; they called themselves Catholic Pentecostals, and I had appointments with them for later in my trip. But I hadn't known that the Jews were also organized.

One night in Berkeley, I was walking along Telegraph Avenue when I came upon a home-made bulletin board affixed to the face of a building. It was covered with layers of announcements, some typed, some mimeographed, some hand-printed, some announcing meetings and rallies, some from people seeking a job or a place to live, some from people offering both, some from people trying to get rid of kittens and puppies. In the lower right-hand corner, under layers and layers of other announcements was the bottom edge of a piece of paper that must have been placed there months before. On it were the words: "Jews For Jesus." What's this? I moistened my fingers and tried to scratch away the layers upon this piece, hoping to find a phone number or an address, but this didn't work. I went into a drugstore and looked for the Jews For Jesus in the telephone directories. No luck. I went into the student lounge at the university and asked around. No luck. I decided I would telephone Jack Sparks in the morning; maybe he would know something.

I didn't come upon any street-witnessing in Berkeley that night, so I went over to North Beach. I strolled along a few blocks, not seeing any Jesus People, and suddenly there they were, five or six of them, young, the girls in long dresses, a few of them carrying the familiar signs—"Jesus Is The One" and "Jesus Is Coming" and "Jesus Loves You." A young man was witnessing to a black youth. The young man was small, swarthy, bearded, and he was dressed as though he were just about to storm San Juan Hill.

I stepped up to one of the girls and asked: "Which group are you?"

She said: "We're Jews For Jesus."

I said: "Praise the Lord! I've been looking for you. Where are you located?"

"In Corte Madera."

"Where's that?"

"On the peninsula."

"Do you have a card or anything?"

She went to the little Rough Rider and spoke to him; he fished a business card out of a pocket and gave it to her; she gave it to me. On it was the name: Moishe Rosen. I wondered if it was the Rough Rider.

Next morning, I called Moishe Rosen for an appointment. I knew immediately it was a different man, an older man. The voice sounded more mature. It also sounded discouraging—not another interview, and to what avail? He told me how to find him, and we met that afternoon. Rosen's office was on the second floor, rear, of a California-type, two-story business building. The suite was modern, neat, unpretentious, like Rosen himself. He was in his early forties, a tall, large man, handsome, greying a bit at the temples and mustache. He was wearing a business suit, but he had the jacket off because the afternoon was warm. The tone I had taken for discouragement turned out to be drollness. Moishe Rosen was a completely charming and witty man.

He had been born and raised in Denver. In 1953, a contact was made between himself and a field agent for the American Board of Missions to the Jews. This was, Rosen told me, an "old line organization," founded in 1894 by Christian Jews for the purpose of bringing Jews to Jesus. After accepting Christ himself, Moishe (Marvin, then) Rosen entered a Bible college in New Jersey. Following his ordination in Denver, the Board assigned him to do missionary work among the Jews of Southern California, converting them.

"Completing them," Rosen put it. "I am a completed Jew. I am more Jewish than I ever was, and I am proud of my Jewishness. A lot of people don't realize that the New Testament is a Jewish book. After all, Jesus is Jewish, too. You know, I have always felt that Jews were natural leaders, only lately they've been leading the wrong things. Look at Abbie Hoffman. Look at Jerry Rubin. They're Jewish. If those two would become Christians, we'd have a couple of new Pauls. They'd be terrific."

I asked: "If your group is supposed to work among

Jews, why, then, last night, were they working on that black boy?"

He shrugged. "These days, you never know. Look at Sammy Davis. Besides, being born in a Christian home doesn't make you a Christian any more than being born in a bakery makes you a bagel. You've got to make the commitment."

In 1957, the Board transferred Rosen from Los Angeles to its headquarters in New York, on West 72nd Street, two blocks from where I was living at the time. Over the years, Rosen worked his way up through the ranks, eventually becoming the second-spot man, as Director of Recruiting and Training. It was a difficult ministry. For a Jew, his religion was not only his religion but it was also his culture. Any frontal attack on him on a religion basis therefore met a double resistance. So it appeared wiser to approach on a cultural basis, demonstrating the Jewishness of Christianity rather than the Christianity of Jewishness. This was done through a variety of ways. Through literature, for one thing, preferably literature that found its way into Jewish homes. Through lectures, for another, usually to Jewish cultural groups. And through lectures, as well, to groups that were neither ethnic nor denominational but a mixed audience of Christians and Jews who had come together on some basis of common interest. All you could hope was that you could plant some seeds of curiosity that would stir some soul-searching in a few people.

The richest fields for completions were college campuses. About eighty percent of the Jews who became Christians via the American Board were college students. Life being as it is in cities, it was possible for a Jewish boy or girl to pass through elementary and high school in a Jewish ghetto, regardless of its socio-economic level, and it wouldn't be until they went away to college that they began to acquire Christian friends. Since people, like water, seek their own level, it often happened that a devout Jew and a devout Christian would become good friends, and sooner or later they would get around to discussing religion. In a campus situation, the American Board field man would usually be more associated with the Christian set, for it was through

Christians that he learned about Jews who were interested enough in religion to discuss it. The day comes, then, when the Christian says to his friend: "Okay, we've reached an impasse, so we need a referee. I know just the man. He'll understand your side because he's Jewish and he'll understand mine because he's Christian." The Jew would wonder how this could be, and the contact was made. Now, there was nothing devious about this. There was no set-ups. Young Christians weren't planted on campus as decoys. Such things would be impossible to pre-arrange, too much of a long shot for the effort.

If the Jew decided to become a Christian—and this did not always happen, his main problem was his family. Rosen told me: "Most of the time, the families aren't really all that Jewish, but they can become very Jewish when it looks like one of the family is turning Christian. I had the experience myself. My wife and I weren't religious. It was a typical Jewish marriage—an agnostic marrying an atheist. Then I became a Christian and I felt the Lord wanted me to go into this ministry, and my wife became so Jewish I expected to see a mezuzah on the door when I got home at night. But my wife is an intelligent woman. I didn't want her to become a Christian for my sake—that never works. But we talked and she read, and her commitment to Christ was her own."

As the New York years passed, Moishe Rosen became increasingly aware of a new force in the country. Youth. Youth was grouping. There were campus demonstrations, sit-ins, protest marches, rallies. There were the drop-outs, the flower children, the hippies, runaways. Underground newspapers. Drugs. Sex.

Rosen told me: "I was as 'Establishment' as anybody could get. I hewed to the 'old line' unswervingly. I grew more and more interested in what was happening to young people and in what they were making happen. A lot of it was ugly, but I felt it was all important, and I wondered if it was all part of a cleansing process. I knew next to nothing about youth work, and I decided to find out what I could. I started hanging around Columbia University and Washington Square, just listening. I had a lot to learn. I began to write articles on my observations; the Board published them, but I could see that everybody around the place was wondering if I had flipped out. I got to know some of the kids; and when I learned that they usually didn't have an indoor place where they could hold meetings, I invited them to use my office. I had a big office on the sixth floor, and before long I had wall-to-wall hippies everyday."

And he did not know what to do with them. Rap sessions were interesting, but they achieved little. Rosen realized that he was approaching the young people on an intellectual level, and he couldn't think of a way to get some action out of them. His work required him to travel a lot, usually not staying in any one place long, and each time his trips took him farther west he'd hear talk about the Jesus People on the Coast.

It was January, 1970, before he got a look at them for himself. He had been invited as a guest lecturer at the Golden Gate Seminary in the Bay Area. At lunchtime, he went into the cafeteria. He told me: "I saw what I thought were three hippies turning on for a bunch of square Baptists. They were talking about the Lord and the Holy Spirit. Now, those students were Christians—after all, they were in a seminary. But they couldn't cope with the hippies, for fire, for aggressiveness, for challenge. Then somebody told me the hippies were Jesus People. I went up to them afterward and told them I'd like to discuss their work with them. They said they'd be on Telegraph Avenue that night, in Berkeley, and would look for me there.

"I'll never forget that night. There were thousands of students strolling the avenue, going into coffee shops and bars and book stores, and in the midst of it all were dozens of Jesus People, carrying their Bibles and their placards, singing, and stopping students and virtually pinning them to the wall, debating with them about what they believed in and how they practiced it and challenging them to commit their lives to the Lord. I got so excited. By the time I got back to New York, my entire orientation had changed. I couldn't sit back and be 'Establishment' anymore. I had to go out into the streets."

Other executives at the American Board didn't think so.

Street-witnessing was not, they pointed out, the Board's way of doing things. Furthermore, one evening on Telegraph Avenue could hardly have made Moishe Rosen an expert in street-witnessing. It could be a fiasco. Rosen conceded that they had a point regarding his experience, so he asked his confreres if they would be willing to compromise by letting him import an expert from California to teach him how to do this thing. They were willing. Rosen sent for Paul Bryant. But Bryant was in college and could not immediately get away for any length of time. The project had to be put off until summer.

That summer day, 1970, when Paul Bryant came walking into the offices of the American Board and identified himself, there was great disappointment everywhere. Though twenty, Paul Bryant was a small, blond young man, and he looked twelve. An expert? A leader? Rosen had forgotten to prepare the office for this turn of events. But what Bryant lacked in quantity, he more than made up for with his peppery enthusiasm. Rosen sent for the nine young Christian Jews who had volunteered for New York's first display of street-witnessing. Counting Rosen and Bryant, they were eleven in all.

One afternoon, they all gathered in Rosen's office, and Rosen asked: "Okay, Paul, what do we do?"

Bryant looked them over. "Is this all you've got?"

"At the moment."

"We ought to do something big," Bryant said. "We have to let people know that we're here. We ought to have a demonstration or a rally, something that'll get in the papers." He looked them over again.

Rosen asked: "And we don't have enough for that?"

"No," said Bryant. "Maybe we can picket something."

"All right," said Rosen. "What?"

"What's the worst part of town?"

"In what way?"

"Well, like North Beach."

"That would be Forty-Second Street," Rosen said.

"Is it bad?"

"Oh, yeah."

"What have they got?"

"Prostitutes of all kinds. Pimps, of course. Pushers. Muggers. Dirty movies. Porno shops."

Bryant said: "Let's picket a porno shop."

"Okay," said Rosen. "What do we do?"

"First we have to make some signs."

"We can do that," said Rosen. They went out and bought some pasteboard and they made the usual signs, that Jesus was coming, that Jesus loved you, that Jesus was the one, and they made several signs knocking pornography. Then they stapled the signs, back to back, so that there would be a message on both sides. Rosen asked: "What do we do now, Paul?"

"We need some wood, some sticks," Bryant said, "something to carry the signs with. Broomsticks are good. Can we get some brooms?"

"We can," said Rosen. They went out and they bought some brooms and they bought a saw and sawed off the brooms. Then they inserted the broomsticks between the pasteboard sheets and stapled the sheets to the broomsticks. Rosen asked: "What do we do now, Paul?"

Bryant said: "Let's go down and try these out."

"Sounds good enough," said Rosen. A storm was coming up. Stiff winds swept in off the Hudson River. As they stepped outside and lifted the signs, the winds ripped the signs off the broomsticks and sent them flip-flopping up the street. They ran after the signs, and when they had gathered them all together, Rosen asked: "What do we do now, Paul?"

Bryant said: "We'll just have to carry the signs by themselves, I guess. How do we get to Forty-Second Street?"

Rosen looked at his watch. It was just five. "The subway would be best."

"Will there be a good crowd there?"

"There will."

There would. Thousands of commuters would be heading westward to the Port Authority Bus Terminal or southward for trains at Penn Station. Thousands more would be heading eastward to their trains at Grand Central. The locals, thousands and thousands of them, would be disappearing down subway stairs or struggling to get up them, with thousands more fighting to get on and off the city buses. There would be the thousands of suburbanites who drove into town each day, now jamming the traffic on the way out. And in the midst of all this would be the Forty-Second Street habitués—who knows how many?—hustling, hustling.

So they all walked east on Seventy-Second Street, the block to Broadway, where the small but famous Needle Park was, and they went down the IRT steps to the narrow platform, and they got on the first downtown express. The train wasn't crowded yet, but it was made so by the large three-by-five-foot signs they carried. Moishe Rosen asked: "What do we do now, Paul?"

Paul Bryant said: "We pray."

"Sounds good enough," Rosen said. So they bowed their heads and they prayed during the non-stop five minute trip to Times Square. Getting off the train was a different matter. The broad Forty-Second Street platform was packed solid. As soon as the train doors opened, a dam-burst of bodies flooded the car. Getting off, with those big signs, demanded the most brutal force. But they got off and they fought their way up onto Forty-Second Street and into the tidal waves of pedestrian traffic. It was beginning to rain.

They had difficulty staying together. Rosen asked: "What do we do now, Paul?"

"We find a porno shop."

They didn't have to look far. Rosen asked: "What do we do now, Paul?"

"Okay," said Bryant. "We keep walking in a circle in front of the place, holding up the signs, and we keep saying 'Down with porno' and 'Don't buy porno' and 'Jesus loves you' and things like that. If we see anybody going into the store, we stop him and rap with him and try to talk him out of it. Okay?"

"Sounds good enough."

They formed a circle but they had trouble staying in it because some of them kept being swept away by the crowds. They held up their signs and they chanted. Moishe Rosen felt a little silly, and he asked the Lord to give him the humility to go through with this. He watched the shop door. Nobody was going in. He hoped that he and his friends were the reason. Five minutes passed. Ten minutes passed. It was beginning to rain harder and the crowds moved faster. Fifteen minutes passed.

A man in his shirtsleeves came out of the store, stopped Rosen and, bewildered, asked: "What the hell is this?"

Paul Bryant stepped up. "We're picketing you."

"What for?"

"For selling pornography."

"What's that got to do with you?"

"We're against pornography."

"That's too bad. Now, get the hell out of here."

"We're staying here until you either stop selling the pornography or we put you out of business."

"Then you're gonna be here a long time. Come on, move on. You're blocking traffic."

Paul Bryant said to Rosen: "Let's go back to work."

Before Rosen could move, the man stopped him again and asked: "What is this? Are you in charge of this?"

Rosen said: "No. He is." And he indicated Bryant.

The man asked: "Well, what kind of a nut are *you?*"

Rosen said: "I'm not a nut. I'm against pornography, too. You're endangering souls."

The man said: "Oh, Christ, a bunch of religious freaks."

Bryant said: "You shouldn't use the name of Jesus Christ like that."

The man said: "What's with Jesus Christ? I'm Jewish."

Rosen said: "So am I."

The man: "Then what are you doing with these crazy kids?"

"I'm a Christian Jew."

"Oh. One of those. Okay. I'm calling the cops." He went inside.

Rosen looked at Bryant. "What do we do now, Paul?"

"This is great," Bryant said. "If the police come, the newspaper reporters won't be far behind. Tomorrow everybody will know that the Jesus People have come to New York. People will start getting in touch with you, and you'll be on your way. Let's get back to work for the Lord." They all resumed picketing.

The call to the police must have gone through fast. In three minutes, two patrolmen assigned to the block came trotting from Eighth Avenue, their walkie-talkies jaggling at their waists. A squad car pulled up. A patrolman asked Rosen: "What's going on here?"

Rosen said: "Officer, we're Christians, and we're picketing this place because they're selling pornography."

"Okay," said the policeman. "Do you have a permit to picket?"

"Do we need one?"

"For something like this, you do."

Rosen looked at Bryant. "What do we do now, Paul?"

"Is there some place around here we can eat?"

"Sure. Lots of places. What do you feel like eating?"

"Just a snack. We've got to kill some time."

They went into a Nedick's and, standing, they ate hot dogs with sauerkraut, washed down with orange juice. They noticed that the paint on their signs was beginning to run. They killed half an hour. Then Rosen asked: "What do we do now, Paul?"

"We go back and picket some more."

"The same place?"

"Yes."

"What if the man calls the police again?"

"We quit too soon, before. We should have waited for the reporters. This time, we stay in there."

"Okay."

The crowds had thinned considerably, and it was raining much harder. They returned to the store and they resumed picketing. This time, the man did not bother to come out. They saw him go quickly, angrily, to his phone. This time, the police did not arrive as fast, and when they did arrive, in ten minutes, they were not the police from the local precinct; they were from the Tactical Force, complete with crash helmets, rifles, machine-guns, smoke bombs, and they came tumbling out of cars, all twenty-five of them, and they surrounded the eleven Jesus People, their weapons drawn and aimed.

Moishe Rosen called: "What do we do now, Paul?"

Paul Bryant called: "Stay in there."

"Okay."

A Tactical sergeant called: "Who's in charge here?" No one answered. The sergeant said: "C'mon, who's ever in charge, raise your hand." They all had their hands raised, holding the signs. The sergeant said: "Well, will somebody tell me what's going on?"

Rosen said: "We're Christians, and we're picketing this store because they're peddling pornography."

The sergeant asked: "Do you have a permit?"

Rosen said: "No. Didn't they tell you?"

The sergeant said: "You can't do this without a permit."

Rosen called: "Paul?"

Bryant called: "Praise the Lord!"

Rosen called: "Praise the Lord!"

A crowd was gathering now. Some people, seeing all the artillery, crossed the street and watched from there.

The sergeant said: "I'm giving you one minute to disband or I'll arrest you all for causing a disturbance and you can praise the Lord all night in jail."

Rosen called: "Paul, are you willing to spend the night in jail?"

Bryant called: "I am, for the Lord."

But a girl in the group called: "My mother will kill me if I have to spend a night in jail, even for the Lord."

Rosen called: "What do we do now, Paul?"

Bryant called: "Is there some place around here we can get dessert?"

"Sure. Is the same place all right?"

"Okay."

So the eleven Jesus People lowered their signs and they walked away. And the twenty-five Tactical policemen lowered their weapons and got back in their cars and rode away.

Paul Bryant was annoyed. "Where were the reporters? They have police radios in their city-rooms. Why didn't they come?"

Rosen consoled: "Usually causing a disturbance on Forty-Second Street isn't very newsworthy."

They went back into Nedick's and they all ordered ice cream cones. The high humidity, caused by the rain, made the cones soggy, and they had to eat the melting ice cream quickly to keep it from running down their arms. Rosen asked: "What do we do now, Paul?"

Paul Bryant looked out the window. It was pouring rain. He looked at the signs. The messages had been rained off. He looked at Rosen. "We could pass out some literature."

"We don't have any literature."

"Then why don't we call it a night?"

"Okay."

Next day, during a conference, Moishe Rosen told his confreres what had happened. Some of them were annoyed; some thought it was hilarious; they all hoped this was the end of it. But Moishe Rosen had had a taste of the battle, and he said: "I know that the Lord wants me to go ahead on this. After all, our ministry is to the Jews, and Jews don't go to Forty-Second Street, so we'll have to look for them somewhere else. I'm sure that the Jesus People method of street-witnessing is right for us, and I want to learn how to apply it to our work. So I'm asking to be relieved of my duties here in New York. I want to go out to San Francisco for a couple of years and learn how to do this right."

To his great surprise, they all approved.

I asked Moishe Rosen why he had settled in such an isolated place, so far from town, in what was little more than a shopping center in the middle of nowhere. He said: "The Lord led me here." And he meant it. He added: "Besides, I have some students in the seminary near here. I think it's a good idea for me to be close to them."

Rosen told me: "My work among Jews would be easier if gentile Christians would start remembering that Jesus is a Jew. The picture of Jesus you find most often in Christian homes shows him with brown hair, blue eyes and a blond beard. Jesus has black hair, black eyes and a black beard; he has a swarthy complexion; he is rather short and stocky. That's the way all Jewish men looked until they started mating with Nordic types centuries later. It is bad enough being blamed for Jesus' death over these past two thousand years, but it is insulting and degrading to be told that Jesus Christ doesn't even look Jewish. This causes an identity crisis in Jews, especially young Jews, which is why a lot of them drift from the faith. A lot of people think that when a Jew becomes a Christian he isn't Jewish any more. That's nonsense. My Jewishness is a part of me the way a black man's skin is a part of him. In accepting Jesus Christ as the Messiah, all I did was acknowledge that I believed everything the prophets wrote about him in the Talmud because the New Testament bore them out."

In the Bay area, Rosen began his ministry by personal witnessing, on the streets and on campuses. Though he addressed himself specifically to Jews, his personal experiences were of general interest, and he held his listeners. Only occasionally was he heckled, sometimes by a Jew who accused him of being a traitor or a Christian who said there was no such thing as a Christian Jew. Some young Jews already in the Jesus Movement heard about Rosen and offered him their aid. He was glad to get it. However, he had no intentions of setting up communes, nor was he interested in acquiring a personal following. In the first place, he didn't know how long he would be in California. Secondly, he was in California for the purpose of learning by doing—New York was still home, and he was being supported from New York. And thirdly, he was a church-oriented man. Any Jews who became Christians through his ministry would, he expected, proceed to lead their normal lives, except now they would be Christian lives, including church-going. Some of the young Jews who became Christians through Rosen's ministry took up wearing the garb of the Jesus People—the long dresses, Rough Rider outfits. Well, that was all right. Rosen was against sectarianism. He didn't want Jews For Jesus to become the Jewish wing of the Movement. Everybody was Christian, and Rosen urged his kids to share in the prayer meetings of other groups. He did, and he also spoke at mass rallies, with Jack Sparks and Linda Meissner, Duane Pederson, the lot.

One day one of Rosen's kids asked him: "How come I always read in the papers about the Christian World Liberation Front, of the Jesus People Army and outfits like that but I never read about the Jews For Jesus?"

Rosen said: "You will."

At the next mass rally, held at San Francisco State College, Rosen showed up with two hundred large posters, one side of each bearing the words JEWS FOR JESUS, the other sides bearing comments like JESUS CAN MAKE YOU KOSHER and YOU DON'T HAVE TO BE JEWISH TO LOVE JESUS. He passed out hundreds of lapel buttons bearing similar legends. He also distributed hundreds of copies of a multi-faced folder, called Jews For Jesus, which he illustrated and hand-printed himself, cleverly and wittily, in which he identified the Jews for Jesus not as a particular movement but as a fact of faith. Next day, Jews For Jesus got dominant coverage in the papers.

That was just the beginning. At North Beach was a strip joint called the Garden of Eden, with topless waitresses to boot. One night in the summer of 1971, Moishe Rosen and some of his kids showed up at the place and started picketing. The doorman tried to get them to leave but he couldn't, so he went for the man in charge.

The man came out, in a huff of anger. "All right," he said. "What's going on here? What do you people want?"

Rosen said: "We want you to change the name of this place."

"You want what?"

"We want you to change the name of this place," Rosen said again. "You call it the Garden of Eden. It is a garden of sin. We want you to change the name."

"You're crazy. Get out of here."

"We're not going anywhere until you change the name."

"Do you want me to call the cops?"

"Go ahead. We'll tell them that you're operating under false pretenses."

"What are you talking about?"

"We're Christians," said Rosen, "and the Garden of Eden is a holy place for us. By calling this place the Garden of Eden, you are deluding people into thinking it is a place of religion."

"That's ridiculous," said the man. "Everybody knows what this place is."

"Not everybody. San Francisco gets a lot of tourists," Rosen pointed out, "and some of them might wander into your place, thinking it is a place where they can pray."

"Oh, come off it," the man said. "Now, come on, you're blocking the door."

"We're nowhere near your door. You won't change the name?"

"No."

"Then we'll give you an alternative," Rosen said. "Put a sign on your door that says this place is not a place of religion."

"Cut it out."

"And put that announcement in your ads, too."

"I'm calling the cops." He turned to leave.

Rosen said: "I'll give you another alternative." The man stopped and looked back. Rosen said: "If you won't change the name and if you won't put up the sign and use the announcement in your ads, we'll stay out here unless you let us go in and witness to your audience."

"Do what?"

"Witness. Talk to them about Jesus Christ."

"I'm calling the cops." And he went inside.

The police never arrived. But the Jews For Jesus arrived at the place night after night, and they were, in fact, just a few feet from the place the night I met them, witnessing as well as protesting. As Moishe Rosen told me about this, he showed me a letter he had recently sent to the owner of the Garden of Eden, again stating the man's choices if he wanted to get the protestors away from the place.

Rosen said: "Look at his name. He's a Jew, yet. That makes things worse. It's a shame, really."

I couldn't be sure whether or not Moishe Rosen was kidding.

But he certainly wasn't kidding about his work. "I love it," he told me. "I'm sure I'm doing exactly what the Lord wants of me. The kids are great. Believe me, there is no such thing as a generation gap. There is no communication gap. But there is an authoritarian gap. For now, the authority is still in the hands of the Establishment, and so life goes on as before—hypocrisy, corruption, war, pollution, racial injustice, all the things the kids are against and have protested against for years, through demonstrations, through violence, through drugs, through dropping out. Well, now they have gotten their heads straightened out through Jesus. They're not always going to be kids. Some day the authority is going to pass into their hands, if only by the act of growing older. They'll know how to use that authority, believe me."

I believed him.

I met Catholic Pentecostals in San Francisco, South Bend and Ann Arbor. Nobody was sure how many Catholic Pentecostals there were in the country, with estimates running from 30,000 to 80,000. With 50 million Catholics in the U. S., this was a sliver, but it could be a sliver that would grow up to become the whole tree.

John Sherrill started it all.

A "cursillo" (Spanish: "little course") is something like a Catholic weekend retreat, except that the retreat rule of silence does not apply, there is layman participation in the teaching, there are group discussions, and both men and women can make a cursillo together. Bishop Juan Hervas, of Spain, founded the *Cursillos de Cristiandad* (short courses in Christianity) in 1949, and the weekends become popular in Europe. In 1952, cursillos began to spread through South America. In 1957, two Spanish air cadets introduced the movement into the U. S., and it caught on quickly, particularly with the age group of young marrieds who usually met while attending Catholic colleges.

To the National Cursillo Convention, of August, 1966, Steve Clark, then on the staff of Saint John's Student Parish in East Lansing, Michigan, took with him a book he had been reading. He didn't quite understand it, and he thought some of his friends might be able to explain it to him. It was *The Cross and the Switchblade*, the Dave Wilkerson story written by John and Tibby Sherrill. The Sherrills wrote the book in a way that Dave Wilkerson's experiences with the Holy Spirit in his life were not explored in detail until the end, and then earlier parts of the book which seemed coincidental or contrived suddenly made sense. But they made sense only if you already knew about the Holy Spirit in the Pentecostal way. Steve Clark gave the book to some friends who were laymen on the faculty of Duquesne University of the Holy Spirit, in Pittsburgh, but they didn't have the time to read the book during the convention and said they'd check with Clark later. When they finally did read the book, they were, like a lot of people, impressed by the evidence of the tremendous influence the Holy Spirit could have in a life once he was invited to do so. They checked out the Bible references in the book, and passages which they felt they already understood now appeared to them in a new light.

Every day for over two months they prayed for the Baptism, but nothing happened. Then one of them, Ralph Keifer, an instructor of theology at Duquesne, came upon John Sherrill's *They Speak With Other Tongues.* And there it was, all spelled out for them. The book indicated that anybody who wanted the Baptism could usually get it by being prayed over by somebody who already had it. Keifer and his friends didn't know anybody who had it, and they were reluctant to make inquiries at Pentecostal churches where they might find somebody who did. Then they remembered an Episcopal priest, Father William Lewis, who had lectured at Duquesne, and they telephoned him and asked him if he had read the Sherrill books. Yes, he had, but he didn't know what to make of them. Did he know anybody who had the Baptism? Yes, he did, a Mrs. Betty Shomaker, a neighbor, and she held prayer meetings at her house every Friday night. He offered to arrange an introduction.

On Friday, January 6, 1967, Keifer and his wife and Patrick Bourgeois, also a theology instructor at Duquesne, attended the prayer meeting at Mrs. Shomaker's house. It was a pleasant and interesting evening, but nothing was said about the Baptism. The following Friday, just Keifer and Bourgeois attended. During the meeting, nothing was said about the Baptism, but after the meeting Keifer and Bourgeois asked Mrs. Shomaker to pray over them. Keifer received the gift of tongues almost immediately; Bourgeois got it later. They went back to Duquesne and started praying over their friends. With that, Catholic Pentecostalism began.

Anybody who criticizes the Jesus People for not having a theology has not met the Catholic wing of the Movement. Besides the coterie of theologians in Pittsburgh, both Kevin and Dorothy Ranaghan, who head the Catholic group in South Bend, have graduate degrees in theology. Dorothy got her bachelor's degree at Duquesne, where she met Keifer and the others; Kevin earned his bachelor's at St. Joseph's Seminary, the major seminary for New York; the Ranaghans met at Notre Dame while working on their master's degree. Another member of the South Bend group is Father Edward D. O'Connor, a professor of theology at Notre Dame, who has written extensively on Catholic Pentecostalism. About half of the group that meets at the University of San Francisco, a Jesuit school, are priests and nuns. The Trappist monks in Kentucky have received the Baptism; so have the Benedictine monks in Iowa. A directory of Catholic groups, published out of South Bend, lists almost 300 of them across the country, and there are priests and/or nuns in all of them. So there are theologians galore.

Every Catholic Pentecostal I met expressed great gratitude to Protestants for the revitalized interest in the Baptism in the Holy Spirit. The Catholic and Protestant leaders of the Movement are friends and have appeared together at seminars and rallies. According to the South Bend directory, many of the Catholic groups have memberships that are as much as 50 percent Protestant. Even so, the Catholics don't consider themselves to be Jesus People in the California sense. For one thing, the Catholics aren't anti-church. In fact, many of them told me that receiving the Baptism had imbued them with a greater love for the church and enhanced their daily devotions. Dorothy Ranaghan told me: "There are still a lot of changes I would like to see in the church, such as the role of women, but I can work better for these changes from the inside than from the outside." Another difference between the Catholics and the Protestants is that the Catholics don't street-witness. It may be for this reason that so few young Catholics, in their mid-teens, are in the Movement. The only place I heard about where addicts had joined a Catholic group in any number was Seattle. In South Bend, the Ranaghans had to stop and think about it, and then Kevin said: "Oh, yes, there has been one. Remember?" He looked at his wife searchingly; Dorothy remembered, but they didn't tell me anything about the person.

Also, the Catholics aren't as concerned about Communism as the Protestants are. Communism came up with every Protestant leader I met—Communists had thrown prayer out of our schools, Communists ran the mass media, they ran the unions, Communist leaders were always being invited to speak on college campuses but no Christians were. Dorothy Ranaghan summed up the Catholic viewpoint when she told me: "I'm not as worried about active Communists as I am about inactive Christians. That's the real problem in this world."

There is also a division of opinion between the Catholics and Protestants on the question of whether we are in the End Times. Every Protestant with whom I discussed this could produce a Bible citation to back up every headline on a front-page as a sign of the Second Coming. But Father Leo Thomas, a Dominican in San Francisco, the Ranaghans in South Bend, and Ralph Martin in Ann Arbor, all theologians, held a different view. Father Thomas said: "Nobody has any knowledge about the historical end of the world. This is information the Father reserved for Himself. We were given some signs, but not much. We are in a period of great change, certainly, and the Holy Spirit is probably more active in the world than he ever was, but we have to be careful not to read between the lines in the Bible. If we were to have this information, it would have been given to us."

Ralph Martin said: "It would be a mistake to write off the Jesus People's emphasis on the End Times. The End Times precede the Second Coming, and this is an important Christian belief. But people can become over-emotional about things like this and make the mistake of misconstruing the signs. Jesus said that even he didn't know when he'd be back, and I don't think we should press it."

And Dorothy Ranaghan said: "I don't know whether we're in the End Times. I do know that *some*thing is happening."

I attended a prayer meeting at Notre Dame. The meeting was preceded by a sort of warm-up for the newcomers, and I attended that, too. Dorothy Ranaghan conducted it. There were about twenty people present, most of them well over thirty. As we went around the room, identifying ourselves, several people turned out to be Protestants and members of Jesus People groups in other towns, here that night either because the Lord told them to come or they were simply curious. One young woman said she was from the Campus Crusade team at another school.

Dorothy Ranaghan began the meeting by saying that she expected everybody was present either because they had the Baptism or they wanted it, and she said: "The Baptism is a gift given only by God to men, not by man to man, although sometimes there is a 'praying over' and laying on of hands. You receive the Baptism as the result of a prayer of faith. You ask Jesus to send the Spirit to you to effect a change in your life. The whole purpose of the Baptism is to praise God. He deserves to be praised, because of who He is and what He is, not what He can do. You will find that your entire spiritual life will be enriched. You will know a sense of calm and joy and love you never experienced before. The Eucharist will remain the heart of your faith, and it will mean more to you than it ever has."

A man who had identified himself as a professor asked: "What are the signs of the Baptism? How do we know we have it? Can we have it without knowing it?"

Dorothy said: "It comes in answer to prayer. The most frequent sign is tongues, though sometimes tongues doesn't happen right away. But you shouldn't look for signs. Look for the fruits of the gift. New peace. New joy. A new desire to read the Scriptures. Don't look for signs. Pray, and then act on it from the start. You should believe without signs."

This opened up a general discussion of people who had the Baptism; they agreed with Dorothy. As the meeting ended, several people signed up for a training course which they would subsequently take for an hour before future prayer meetings.

The prayer meeting was held in a large room on the second floor, with about 150 people present, perhaps twenty of them priests and nuns. The Ranaghans told me later it was a slow night. We sat on folding chairs arranged by rows in a large circle. In the center sat a young woman with a guitar. The Ranaghans sat near her. Somebody had a tambourine. The meeting was conducted by a young man who was, I learned later, a conscientious objector and had chosen, as his alternate service, to work as a hospital orderly. He was also active in the campus apostolate—the Catholic equivalent to Campus Crusade. He was a very soft-spoken young man, and he seemed shy. He started us off with several hymns; they were the same hymns that the Jesus People sang. The singing was good, better than I had ever heard at anything Catholic, though not as full-voiced and boldhearted as those kids at Calvary Chapel.

Then there was silence. I waited, wondering. I began to hear tongues around me, softly. I watched the Ranaghans. Their heads were bowed in prayer. Then a woman stood up, and she said: "I have brought you together to gather you in one flock, one flock faithful to me. I call upon you to be faithful to my son. His blood was shed for you. He is here. I have come to be in your midst. Free yourselves of your burdens. Tell others of your love for me."

People muttered "Praise the Lord" and "Praise Jesus" and "Praise God."

This, then, had been prophecy. We had heard the woman's voice, but it wasn't she who was speaking. It was God speaking through her. I'd heard prophecy once before, but in tongues. This was at Lyle Stennis's church. Breck Stevens was up there, preaching at full blast, when an elderly woman, Mexican, perhaps Indian, began to speak in tongues loudly. Breck stopped, bowed his head and clasped his hands at his chest. All the people in the church bowed their heads. From the stage, still sitting at the drums, Stennis interpreted as the woman spoke. She said just about the same thing as the South Bend woman, except that her message added that we were in the End Times and the Second Coming would occur soon. At South Bend, two or three others prophesied, all with a similar message.

And there was some witnessing. One man told how receiving the Baptism had saved a marriage that he knew about. The couple had been married three or four years and had reached the point where they could not be in the same room without open combat. One evening the wife went with friends to a prayer meeting, and she received the Baptism. When she got home, her husband couldn't recognize her, she was so loving. He thought it was a trick, but after she kept it up for several days and explained what had happened, he decided to go to a prayer meeting. He did, he got the Baptism, and they were living happily ever after.

A young man got up, and he said: "A couple of weeks ago, I was driving in from the country, and I passed this car at the side of the road. I glanced in it as I went by, and it seemed to me that the man at the wheel was having trouble getting it started, even though it was a new car. I kept on going, and then I began to get this feeling that I ought to go back and see if I could help the man. The feeling kept getting stronger and stronger, and I must have gone ten miles before I turned around and headed back. Sure enough, there he was, only he was out looking under the hood. I stopped and I went over to him and I asked if I could help him. He said he couldn't get the car started and he didn't know enough about cars to figure out what was wrong. Well, I don't know that much about cars, either. I knew there wasn't a garage or phone for miles, so I offered to drive the man to the nearest garage or I could stop off myself and send somebody to him. He said he'd better stay with his car. So I headed back to my car and—I don't know why—I stopped and turned and I said: 'Hey, mister, do you mind giving me your name and address?' He told me. I got into my car and headed back into town and I stopped off at the first garage I came to and told the attendants about this man, and one of them got into the tow truck and headed out there. I praised the Lord for letting me be helpful to my brother, and then I forgot about it.

Well, for a couple of days, something was bugging me and I couldn't figure out what it was. Then, out of a clear sky, I remembered that man's name and address. Next thing I knew, I was putting some literature about us into an envelope and I was writing him a note about where he could find some Catholic Pentecostals near him, if he was interested. Then I did forget about it. Until yesterday. He called me. They were Catholics and they did go to a prayer meeting and they signed up for the training, and the other night he and his wife were praying at home and they got the Baptism. So that's how the Lord used me to help this man in a real way."

People muttered "Praise the Lord" and "Praise Jesus" and "Praise God."

Then silence. Tongues, again. Someone, a woman, the guitarist, I thought, sang in tongues, and it was pleasant to hear. The meeting seemed totally unstructured. People got up and witnessed or prophesied or made a comment or called out the number of a hymn they wanted the group to sing or prayed in tongues or just sat there, however the Spirit moved them, and this went on for over two hours. Then the young man conducting the meeting gave a short talk, on how we should always praise God and ask Him to use us for His purposes. Then he said a prayer, in English, people around me joining him in tongues, we sang another hymn, and that was it. The meeting, it seemed to me, was very much like a Jesus People meeting, except that it was calmer and shorter and the people were not as young.

It was perhaps because of the age of the Catholics that they were able to proceed on one of the most impressive features of the Jesus Movement. It was the complete return to Christian living as it was first lived. Acts 2, 44-47 says: "And all who believed were together and had all things in common; and they sold their possessions and goods and distributed them to all, as any had need. And day by day, attending the temple together and breaking bread in their homes, they partook of food with glad and generous hearts, praising God and having favor with all the people. And the Lord added to their number day by day those who were being saved."

The leading proponent of this kind of life for today's Christians was Ralph Martin. An Easterner, born in New York and raised in New Jersey, Martin told me that he had always felt a call to some role in the religious life, though he was sure it wasn't the priesthood. In 1960, he entered Notre Dame as a freshman. Martin was with Steve Clark when, in August, 1966, Clark took the copy of *The Cross and the Switchblade* to the Cursillo convention. They were both working in East Lansing then, but later moved to Ann Arbor to work with students at the University of Michigan. After the Pittsburgh group came into the Spirit in 1967, Clark and Martin received the Baptism.

But Ralph Martin told me: "I'm sure I received the Baptism before that. In 1964, I was down in the dumps for some unknown reason, and I was ready to drop the whole religion scene. Then a friend talked me into a Cursillo weekend. I had a terrific spiritual experience that weekend. I started speaking in a language I didn't understand; I didn't know what it was—tongues, so I stopped it."

When I met him, Martin was editor of "New Covenant," a monthly magazine for Catholic Pentecostals, and "covenant" was the key word in the Christian life he advocated and, in fact, was living. In theology, a covenant is the promise by God to bless those who obey Him or fulfill some other condition. For example, God made a covenant with the Jews, that He would lead them out of Egypt and to the Promised Land in return for their obedience. God kept His part of the bargain, but the Jews didn't keep theirs. In Jeremiah, God says that He will be willing to make a new covenant with the Jews, in which: "I will set my laws in their understanding and write them on their hearts; and I will be their God, and they shall be my people. And they shall not teach one another, saying to brother and fellow-citizen, 'Know the Lord!' For all of them, high and low, shall know me; I will be merciful to their wicked deeds, and I will remember their sins no more." In his letter to the Hebrews, Paul quoted Jeremiah, and then he went on to tell the Hebrews that Jesus Christ was the mediator of the new covenant and they should hold fast to their faith in him.

But there is another type of covenant, which is a pact, an agreement, by a number of people to adhere to the specifications of the agreement. Among the Catholic Pentecostals, the agreement—the covenant—is to live in community, holding all things in common. One of Ralph Martin's axioms is: Christianity is essentially communal, and yielding to God must mean yielding to a community form of life. Martin is convinced that the Jesus Movement will fizzle out unless Christians enter the communal way of life. By this, he does not mean the type of communes I visited in California, in which a number of young people, most of them recently off drugs, live together—and apart—until they become spiritually strong enough to face the world. In a covenant, the commitment is for life, it is a part of life, active in life, and growing. Members of a covenant take on full responsibility for each other—spiritually, socially, economically, for better or worse, in sickness and in health, until death.

When I met the Ranaghans, they were a week away from entering a covenant with about twenty other people, and they had just moved in order to be closer to the other members. Dorothy told me: "This is going to be a real test in Christian love. I'm like anybody else: I prefer to associate with my peers. We have people in our covenant who hold doctorates, but we also have some who didn't finish grammar school. Kevin and I didn't make a list of our twenty best-liked friends for the covenant; this group just happened to be together one night when the Spirit moved us to form the covenant. Well, you don't choose your brothers and your sisters, but you love them. It has to be the same in a covenant."

Members of a covenant try to live as close to each other as they can. Often there are at least two families living in the same house; several families may share apartments in the same building. Protestants are in the covenants; and although Protestants and Catholics worship in the Spirit together, they also go to their own churches. The covenant is considered by all to be Catholic at the core. For the

Catholics, living together means they are also members of the same parish, and this gives them a further sense of community. All members of a covenant must have received the Baptism.

Everybody in the covenant who can work does work, sometimes within the community as administrators or in supply and maintenance. With the exception of professional people—doctors, lawyers, architects, people whose work usually requires long-term involvement—the members prefer religion-affiliated jobs—teaching religion in schools, the campus apostolate, working at office jobs at the parish or diocesan levels, publishing. All earnings go into a common kitty, and the kitty is tithed. Individual needs are met as they come up.

Members of a covenant are also active in the community around them—getting people better acquainted so they can get along better, running a day-care center for the children of working mothers, visiting the sick, helping the poor, counseling on personal and spiritual matters. In South Bend, one covenant settled down in the black ghetto, where there were a lot of problems, and their homes virtually became the community center.

Besides the total commitment to the service of the Lord, the idea of a covenant is growth as a spiritual force. It stands to reason that a community where a covenant is established will feel the effects of it, with more covenants growing out of it. However, an aspirant does not move into a covenant simply because he has the Baptism and wants to try the life. As happened in Ann Arbor, the pioneers in the living-together groups had two or three years of experience in Catholic Pentecostal leadership behind them before they decided to take this step. Those who followed them had similar backgrounds of experience and training. Ralph Martin told me: "Living together like this requires great love, wisdom and tact. We all have our faults. Part of the experience of living together is to learn about our faults and correct them. This means we must be honest with each other, and this presents some of the biggest problems in community life. To speak the truth without love is destructive, but to love without speaking the truth can be equally disastrous."

Wherever I went on my trip, I saw evidence of activity and growth and peace and love. In Ann Arbor, in addition to all of these, I saw evidence of something else. I saw evidence of permanence.

8

Tales Of Six Cities

Carl Parks told me: "The only thing worse than being a minister's son is when the minister is your mother." Both of Parks' parents were ministers in the Assembly of God Church, but his father died when Carl was a year old. His mother was a popular revivalist, which meant a boyhood of almost constant travel for Carl Parks, and this meant that the boy had difficulty making any progress in school.

Carl was twelve when his mother was finishing a revival in Lewiston, Idaho, and preparing to move on again, and one day he said to her: "Why don't we find some place around here for me to live so I can go to school? We have some friends here and they can keep an eye on me, and when you have any time off you can come back here and rest." The woman knew the boy was right. They located a furnished apartment and, at the ripe old age of twelve, Carl Parks was on his own.

It was also at the age of twelve that Carl Parks received the Baptism at one of his mother's services, and he spoke in tongues.

Despite this, Parks grew up only as a nominal Christian. He had too much freedom as a boy. He said: "I was into everything except drugs. What saved me was that I married young."

In 1969, at thirty-one, Carl Parks was living in Spokane, Washington. He had a good marriage, five nice kids, he owned his own home, and he also owned a new Mercedes-Benz. He was doing very well as the regional representative of the LaSalle Extension School, selling correspondence courses. That October, Parks was summoned to the main office, where he was offered a vice-presidency at a salary of $36,000 a year, but he would have to move out of Spokane. They gave him three months to think it over. He knew the answer before he got out of the building. He was going to take the job.

Then something happened. He was on the plane, flying home, when he distinctly heard the words: "Don't take that job because it will cost you your soul." He looked at the man next to him; the man was asleep. But Carl knew the voice had come from within himself, and he didn't know what to make of it. He tried to put the memory of it out of his mind. Then he heard it again: "Don't take that job because it will cost you your soul."

When he got home and told his wife about the offer, she asked: "Are you going to take it?"

He said: "I don't know."

For three months, he could not make up his mind. At times he would daydream about all that money and living in the East; but just when he'd start getting comfortable with himself, something disquieting would stir deep in his heart, and he would be filled with uncertainty again. He did not hear the voice again but he could not forget it, and he would not concede to himself that it might have been God.

The deadline approached. Parks sent a letter to the main office. He said he did not want to leave Spokane, and so he was resigning as of the first of the year.

He had no idea what he was going to do with himself. He had a little money in the bank, but with five kids a little money wasn't going to last long. He knew he would have to get a job. He read the ads for salesmen, but nothing interested him. Two months passed this way. And during the two months, something else was happening to him that he could not understand. He felt a slowly growing desire to read the Bible. He had not touched a Bible since he was eighteen and had graduated from high school and quit going to Sunday School. But now there was this urge.

One day he asked his wife: "Do we have a Bible around here?"

"Of course we have," she said. "It's in your office."

He could not remember ever seeing it.

He went into his office and he shut the door and he found the Bible and he sat down at his desk and began to page through the book. Parks told me: "I couldn't figure out what was happening—me, reading the Bible, after all these years. I thought I was going nuts. Then something hit me—I'll never forget it; it was March 6—and I got this terrific desire to kneel down and pray. I knelt down and I prayed like I'd never prayed before in my life. I spent three weeks in that room, hardly ever going out, just reading the Bible and praying. I slept in there, and often I'd awake during the night, and I'd read and pray. When I finally walked out of that room, I was a different man. I was totally committed to the Lord. Only I didn't know as what."

Easter came. Carl Parks took his family into Seattle for the holidays. Linda Meissner's Jesus People Army was running all over the place proclaiming the resurrection of the Lord. Parks got into conversations with some of the kids. They asked him if he were a Christian. Yes. Had he been saved? Yes. Had he received the Baptism? Before they were born. They told him about Linda and her coffeehouse and they invited him over. He went there. He met Linda, and they talked. Before Carl Parks got back to Spokane, he knew exactly what he was going to do with his life.

"The Lord always seemed to be a step ahead of me," Parks said, grinning boyishly at the thought. "I knew a man here in Spokane who had done some time on minor offenses. About a year before, he was in the local jail, awaiting sentencing to the penitentiary, and he committed his life to Jesus and he was saved. In the penitentiary, he brought a lot of the inmates to the Lord, and it got into the papers. Just before we left for Seattle, I heard that he was out. When I got back, I looked him up because I wanted him to work with me on the kids. He told me that he was already in the process of opening a coffeehouse for the hippies so that he could talk to them about the Lord. I didn't even know we had any hippies in Spokane. We had hundreds. So we opened up the place, and we started getting converts the first night.

"It was the same when we started needing housing. About half our hippies were locals and the rest were gypsies. When the gypsies got the Baptism, they needed a place where they could live and study. It happened so many times. I'd see an ad in the paper for a house for rent; I'd look the place over and tell the people what I wanted to use the place for; they'd say no, they didn't want the house turned into a commune. I'd leave, and before I'd reach my car, the people next door would come out of their house and ask me if I still needed a place, and I'd take it.

"One of our houses got pretty crowded, and we agreed that the married couples should have a house of their own. We wanted the house to be close by because this was a good group and we wanted them to stay together. Even before we started looking, the people across the alley came over and told us that they had to go out of town for a couple of years and did we want to rent their house, fully furnished.

"The same thing happened when we needed a bus. There were a lot of little towns around here that had no contact with the Jesus kids, so we'd borrow as many cars as we could, pack them, and go out to as many Main Streets as we could in a day. We were spending a lot of money on gas. We knew we needed a bus. Do you know what a new bus costs? Have you any idea what a second-hand bus costs? It seemed out of the question. Then one day I saw an ad in the paper for buses. A man who owned a bus company had bought a fleet of new buses and was willing to sell the old ones for thirty-three hundred dollars. Now, that's very cheap. I went over there and inspected the buses, and they were in good shape. But all I could raise was three thousand dollars. So I asked the man if he would settle for three thousand dollars in cash, then and there. He settled.

"The Lord did another wonderful thing for us. We wanted to have a big rally, and we knew that the best way to attract a big crowd was to have some good music. The best rock group in the Northwest is Wilson McKinley. I got in touch with them and asked them how much they wanted to play at our rally. Their price was very heavy, but I knew that we needed them and I said okay. Well, all four guys got caught up in the spirit of the rally and they were converted. Not only did they refuse to take a cent for the rally, but they joined our team. They've appeared with us all over the West."

Enthusiasm bubbled out of him.

In order to equip himself better for the work he was doing, Carl Parks took a crash course at a Bible college in Illinois, and he was ordained. Parks' attitude toward his kids was less long-range than other leaders. When they have a solid enough Christian foundation, he prefers that they go back home. However, many of them have wanted to remain in the Movement, and he has backed them in starting other Jesus People colonies in Northwest towns.

One of the ideas which Linda Meissner and Carl Parks agreed upon was that the Northwest needed a newspaper of its own. Though Parks knew nothing about publishing, he said he would start one. He found a staff among his people, kids who had studied journalism or art in high school or college. They called the paper *Truth*. It turned out to be more of a newspaper than, say, the *Hollywood Free Paper,* which is more of a psychedelic happening; *Truth* has a professional look and tone.

When the first issue was ready, the kids rushed downtown to start passing it out. They came back in a huff. One boy said: "Do you know what people did? We'd give them the paper, they'd look at it and see that it was about the Jesus People, and they'd drop it on the sidewalk."

"Then don't give the paper away," Parks said. "Ask for a donation. People don't throw away what they've paid for." It worked.

The people on the staff do not get paid for their work. Carl Parks does not draw any salary from any aspect of his work. I asked him how they all managed to survive.

"The paper pays for itself now," he said. "The rest just comes in. We don't ask anybody for it. We don't ask the Lord for it. The Lords knows what we need. He provides."

Tom Rozof became the leader of the Jesus kids in Wichita, Kansas, because one day his car broke down there. It wasn't even his car. With two friends, Tom had left California on a cross-country trip to distribute a religious newspaper called *Good News*. The car belonged to one of the other boys. According to Tom Rozof: "It was a 1919 Nash. We couldn't go any faster than thirty-five miles an hour, we got about seven miles on a gallon of gas, and we had to push the thing a lot." It was a crazy thing for them to do, but they were young and filled with the Spirit, eager to witness from coast to coast.

Tom Rozof was born and raised in the Los Angeles area. He came from a Catholic family and went to Catholic schools. He told me: "I did all the things a Catholic boy is supposed to—daily Mass, Communion, the rosary, the works, but, looking back, I know I wasn't having a personal relationship with Christ." He loved music, folk music. He took guitar lessons and became good enough to get jobs with groups that wandered through the mountains looking for gigs at resort inns. After high school, he went into music full-time. But the jobs were not full-time, so he was on unemployment compensation more than he was off it. He was also on to drugs, starting with pot, then progressing to hash, acid and speed. He was also on to liquor and sex. He no longer lived at home.

He knew he was killing himself, but he could not bring himself to straighten out. Sometimes weeks went by when he had no idea where he was or what he was doing. When he'd return from these trips, he felt rotten, disgusted with himself. He considered suicide. One day he became so desperate that he decided to go to confession, hoping that would help. In the dark cubicle, when he finished reciting the frequency of his sins over the past three or four years, he heard the priest tell him how many prayers to say as penance.

Tom said: "Father, I don't want to live like this anymore. I know I'm killing myself. But I don't know how to change."

The priest said: "Try harder."

When he told me this, Tom Rozof looked away and smiled sadly. Then he looked back at me challengingly and he said: "As though you can do it yourself."

Early in 1970, when Tom Rozof was twenty-one, he, a few friends and a couple of girls were living in a shack in the mountains, trying to find work at the ski resorts. They were running low on drugs, and one of the boys announced that he was going into Fresno to get a fresh supply. What he got was a supply of Jesus Christ. Some Jesus People had cornered him on a Fresno street, out-talked him, led him to a prayer meeting, and there, while he was on his knees, bewildered by all that was going on around him, he received the Baptism. He stayed with the Jesus kids two weeks, and when he went back to the mountains, all he took with him was a Bible. As he entered the shack, he announced: "I'm gonna straighten you people out."

All day he talked to them about what had happened to him in Fresno, about the Baptism, about the fact that he had not had a fix in two weeks and did not want one, about the terrific kids he had been staying with, about what they believed, about what he now believed. They sat there, staring at him, listening to him in disbelief. Hours passed, and nobody thought to suggest a break for food. Night fell, and nobody moved to turn on a light. Then the boy told them all to kneel, and he taught them how to pray, and he moved among them, touching them, as he softly prayed in tongues.

A jolt of joy shot through Tom Rozof. He had never reached such a high before in his life. He felt an urge to laugh, but he knew that if he moved a muscle he would burst into tears. A girl started to mumble unintelligibly. Tongues. The boy had said it would happen. Tom waited for it to happen to him. Nothing. All day, Tom had had reservations as he listened to the boy. This wasn't religion as he had been taught it. Religion was Mass and the sacraments and Lent. Tom knew next to nothing about the Scriptures; so much of what the boy had pointed out to them had been news to Tom, some of it meaningless. Even as he had knelt on the boy's orders, he was not sure about all this. Now it didn't matter. Something great had happened to him. He felt wonderful. Wow.

They stayed at the shack another two weeks, studying. What they couldn't get over was that none of them had any desire for drugs. Tom didn't even feel like smoking a cigarette. They all knew that, in a cupboard, was a full bottle of wine and a bottle of whiskey with about three drinks in it. Nobody touched the stuff. And they didn't discuss it, but they all knew that the sex had stopped. And they were happy.

Then they went to Los Angeles and they found a house that had enough bedrooms for each to have his—and her—own. They made contact with Jesus People so that they could get some guidance on their development. And they all went on unemployment. One day Tom went to pick up his unemployment check, and he stopped himself at the door.

"No," he said aloud. "I'm not going to do this anymore, either. I'm going to work. I'm going to earn my living even if I have to cut grass." He did cut grass. He waxed cars. He mopped floors. He washed dishes. He earned his own living.

It was in October that Tom Rozof and his two friends

decided to cross the country for the Lord, supporting themselves by selling the religious newspaper. They made it to the Chicago area, where they ran out of papers, ran out of money, and ran out of the desire to see the Atlantic Ocean. They had been told they would find a welcome at Wheaton College, in the Chicago suburbs, and they did, staying there a few days, resting, before starting the long journey back to California. As they were leaving, they were given a list of names of people along the way who would also welcome them if they needed any help.

One night, in Iowa, they parked at the side of the road for the night and they slept in the car. In the middle of the night, Tom Rozof awoke and decided to stretch his legs. It was while he was walking down the dark road, alone in the cold night, that he began to speak in tongues. It was a quiet experience. Very peaceful.

A few days later, as they were approaching Wichita, the 1919 Nash broke down again, this time beyond repair. They checked their list of friends-along-the-way and found Bob Myers, pastor, Faith Presbyterian Church, Wichita. They phoned him, and Myers invited them for dinner. All evening they talked about the Jesus Movement on the Coast and what it was achieving with kids.

Myers became keenly interested. "I wish we could start something like that around here," he said. "We've got a drug problem, of course. More than that, the young people just aren't coming to church. I don't know what they're looking for. Maybe it's what you've got. Would you fellows consider staying around for a while, and see if you can get the Movement going in Wichita?"

Tom Rozof was willing, but the other two had to get back to California. "I figure I can stay about a month," Tom said.

Myers said: "Thanks, Tom. I'll make an announcement in church Sunday morning. We can hold the first meeting some night next week."

The announcement was made on Sunday. On the night of the first meeting, six kids showed up. It was very disappointing. The next week there were ten; the next, a dozen; the last, twenty.

Tom decided to hitchhike back to California. Bob Myers drove him to the edge of town. Tom said: "Well, at least you've got something started. I'm disappointed by the turn-out, though. We should have gotten more kids than that."

"Maybe we should have done some street-witnessing," Myers suggested.

"Your kids aren't ready for that," Tom said. "What we should have done was try to make contact with more and more kids. We should have gone where the kids were."

"Where?"

"The schools, maybe."

"That's an idea."

"It's worth trying."

They said good-bye.

In California, Tom Rozof felt strangely uneasy, and he could not figure out what was bugging him. He tried to apply himself to his studies, to the Movement, to his variety of odd jobs, and yet he couldn't keep his mind on whatever he was doing. Then one night, several weeks later, he got a telephone call from Bob Myers, and Myers said: "Tom, you've got to come back here. The kids keep asking about you, when you're coming back. We've got around fifty kids now, but the new ones have come because they heard about you. This is your program, Tom, and you've got to run it."

Tom said: "Gee, Bob, I don't know. I'm not sure how long I could stay, and I wouldn't want to start anything I couldn't finish."

Myers asked: "Do you have any definite plans for your future?"

"Not really."

"Well, then, Tom," Myers said, "this kind of work will never be finished. There'll always be new kids coming along with new hang-ups. Why don't you just come back to Wichita and start calling it home."

"You mean live there?"

"Why not?"

"I don't know," said Tom. "I haven't thought of that. Why don't we put out a fleece on it?"

"The fleece has already been put out," Myers said firmly.

"What was it?"

"Your car fell apart here, didn't it?" Myers challenged. "Now, are you going to settle for that or are you going to be like Paul and have the Lord knock you off a horse before you recognize what he wants you to do?"

Tom said: "I'll leave here tomorrow."

Tom said to me: "The Lord put me here."

He resumed where he had left off. The high schools let him address assembly meetings. At the next prayer meeting, a hundred kids showed up; at the next, over two hundred; in a few weeks, there were five hundred. Not only did the kids attend the prayer meetings, with all the singing, but they attended Bible classes, and they did their homework.

Tom Rozof introduced an innovation I didn't find anywhere else in the country. He explained: "I knew that parents and kids have problems with each other, and I didn't want religion to become a problem. I was sure it would be just as big a shock to parents to hear their kids become Bible-quoters overnight as it would be to find out the kids were pushers or prostitutes. I knew that having the kids pray in tongues around the house was going to cause a lot of trouble.

"At first, when the kids were coming in so fast, it was impossible for me to go to their homes and meet their parents on an individual basis. So we had some meetings at the church for parents only, and I explained everything. Later on, when things leveled off, as new kids came in, I'd have a talk with them and then go to their homes and have a talk with their parents. The parents are really with the Movement here in Wichita. In fact, some of the parents have formed their own prayer groups and many of them have received the Baptism. We may be the only Jesus People group in the country with a P.T.A."

Rozof was a church-oriented man. He said: "A church is of God. If the Movement is of God, then it should also be of the church. I know that some churches won't let the Jesus kids in. Okay, so they can go find another church. It's Christianity we're concerned about, not denominations of it."

On his own role in the church, Tom Rozof held no strong view. He was not an ordained minister when I met him. He said: "I believe that God ordains ministers, not men, and so maybe I'm already ordained. As things are, in this state I can baptize and marry people. I just don't want to be away from my kids for as long as it takes to go through a seminary and be ordained. Some ministers in town are trying to arrange an ordination for me without that. If it works out, fine; if not, that's okay. I know my Bible. The Holy Spirit has opened it up for me. We are doing the Lord's work, and it is going very well."

I asked him: "How do you account for that?"

He said: "The Lord is trying harder."

David Rose became the leader of the Jesus kids in Kansas City because of a vision.

Rose was born in Independence, Missouri, the ninth in a family of ten children. In his early years, he felt he was not getting enough attention around the house, that he was not loved, and he compensated for this by daydreaming all kinds of dramatic adventures for himself. When he was fourteen, his family went to Hollywood on a vacation, and they took tours of the movie and television studios. Beholding all that glamor, David Rose discovered what he was going to do with his life. He was going to become an actor. Looking back, Rose felt later that the Holy Spirit first entered his life when he was fifteen: the boy felt a calling to the ministry. But he was quite sure that he was the most sinful person in the world and could not possibly have a valid vocation. He put the thought out of his mind.

At 16, he was graduated from high school, and he ran away from home. To Hollywood. This time, he wasn't a tourist, and it was not as easy for him to get into the movie and television studios. Completely untrained and with no knowledge of agents and casting directors and unions, he lost a lot of time trying to get past doormen at the studios. He finally gave up. He wandered out to Newport Beach and became a surf bum. He went on drugs. He became a pusher. A year passed.

For no reason at all, he drifted up to San Francisco, still

pushing. One day he made the mistake of trying to sell some pot to an agent. He was arrested, he was arraigned, he was released on bond. He spent a year around San Francisco, still pushing as he waited for his trial. To his astonishment, charges against him were dropped. The only explanation he could imagine for it was, as he told me: "I was scared stiff. I prayed. When I thought about this later, I wondered why God should answer prayers from somebody like me."

He returned to Los Angeles. By day, he slept on the sand at Newport Beach. By night, he strolled the Strip, buying, selling, boozing, making out. One night, somebody thrust a tract into his hand. He knew what it was, and holding it was like being scalded. He jammed it into his pocket. Then he did something he had never done before. For the first time, he walked slowly along the Strip, and he looked at people. He really looked at people. He saw loneliness. He saw pain. He saw sorrow. He saw fear. He saw hate. He saw despair. He saw slow suicide.

Shaking and puzzled, he turned into a sidestreet and went a few steps. He stopped. He looked around. He was in front of Arthur Blessitt's *His Place*. He went in. Nothing particular happened to David Rose that night, and he stayed less than an hour. He listened to some witnessing, though not too attentively; he eavesdropped on some rapping, not attentively. He went back to the beach for the night. Next night, he was at *His Place* again, this time for three hours. Some of the witnessing struck him as interesting, mostly because the lives which people were acknowledging had been so much like his own. Wasted. The rapping was interesting, too. Some of the guys really knew their Bible. He went back to the beach.

Next day, when he awoke, there was a young man sitting on the sand a short distance from him, watching him. Seeing that Rose was awake, the young man said: "Hi."

Rose said: "Hi."

The young man asked: "How you doing?"

"I'll live."

"Good. Haven't I seen you at *His Place?*"

"The coffeehouse?"

"Yes."

"Maybe."
"You go there much?"
"I've been there twice."
"Why?"
Rose shrugged. "Something to do."
"Do you dig that scene?"
"What?"
"Oh, Jesus and the Holy Spirit and all that."
"Not much."
"Are you a Christian?"
"I doubt it."
"How old are you?"
"Nineteen, soon."
"Any college?"
"Just high school. Why the interview?"
"I'm with Campus Crusade for Christ."
"What's that?"
"We train people to work on college campuses, bringing Christ to the students and bringing the students to Christ."
"What are you doing here, then?"
The young man dodged the question. "Have you ever thought of doing anything like that?"
"No."
"You've never considered any kind of ministry?"
"Not really."
"Not really?"
"When I was a kid, I thought I was being called into the ministry, but that fizzled out."
"It's not too late."
"You're kidding."
"No, I'm not. You're not going to spend the rest of your life sleeping on beaches, are you? You've got to do something with your life."
"I've got time to worry about that."
"Maybe you don't. Now, listen to me," the young man said, intently. "I saw you last night at *His Place,* and the night before, and I knew you were new. Both nights I felt that the Lord wanted me to go over to you and talk to you about Campus Crusade because he wanted you to join. But both nights you looked so uptight that I didn't want to get

the brush, so I decided to wait a few more nights, until you got used to the atmosphere. Now, when I left my home this morning I head east because I was due for an important meeting at our headquarters at Arrowhead Springs. Somewhere along the way, I made a wrong turn, and I found myself going southwest. Well, I've made the trip to headquarters so often that I can drive it with my eyes closed. So when the Lord plays a trick on me like this, there's nothing I can do but go along with him. I had no idea what he wanted me to do. I wasn't even thinking about you. But when I got here and started walking down the beach and I saw you lying there asleep, then I understood. I don't know why, but Jesus wants you."

David Rose couldn't believe this. He asked: "How do I know you're not making all this up?"

"Why should I? I'm two hours late now for a meeting that's important for the Lord, so only the Lord could keep me from it," said the young man. "How about it? Are you going to say no to the Lord?"

Rose looked away, thinking: "Lord, the last time I prayed to you, you kept me out of jail. I don't know when's the last time I prayed before that or what happened. I'm praying now. If you want me to go with this dude, Lord, you're going to have to clear the road." He looked back at the young man. "I don't have any money."

"You don't need any."

"I don't know the Bible."

"We'll teach you."

"I'm an addict."

"Jesus will cure you."

"I've been busted."

"So was he."

Rose felt he was drowning. In anguish, he asked: "Why me?"

"I don't know," said the young man. "You'll have to ask the Lord. All I was supposed to do was find you."

David stood up. "Where is this place?"

David Rose was in his fourth day of training at Campus Crusade when he realized that he had not used drugs for five days. He had been unable to go a day without drugs for almost three years. Shortly after this, David Rose began to pray in tongues.

Finishing his training as Rose was beginning his was Jack Sparks, and they became friends. Sparks told Rose what kind of work he wanted to do at Berkeley. As Rose was finishing his eight weeks of training, he wrote Sparks and asked if he could join him. Sparks invited Rose to live with his family in Oakland. Later, as Sparks was able to open communes in Berkeley, Rose became the elder of one of them, and the two men worked together for eighteen months.

Then David Rose had his vision. He told me:

"It was night. I was in bed, but I've never been sure whether I was awake or asleep. A scene appeared in front of me. It was a building, like the Parthenon, a big one, as big as the Empire State. It looked unreal, like a painting. As I was watching it, the building began to fall apart. It started crumbling. Pieces of it were falling to the ground. Then the scene changed. I saw a lot of people at a party, and they were all smoking pot. They were the ugliest people I ever saw, worse than that night on the Strip. And pieces of the building were falling all around them. Then I saw myself in the scene, at the party. I was walking around and talking to the people. And as I was talking to them, they turned beautiful, really beautiful, and the pot disappeared from the scene. Pieces of the building kept falling all around, but nobody got hit. Then I saw the Lord, and I asked him: 'What place is this?' And he said: 'Kansas City.' Outside the scene, in my room, for real, I heard myself say: 'I'm going to Kansas City.' And the Lord looked at me and said: 'I'll go with you.' "

Next day, he told Jack Sparks about the vision, although he was willing to concede that it may have been a dream. Sparks said: "What's the difference? An angel appeared to Joseph in a dream and told him that Mary was going to have a child. Dream or vision, Dave, if you think it was a message from the Lord for you to go to Kansas City, then you should go." He went. En route, he stopped off at Arrowhead Springs to marry Toni, whom he had met at Campus Crusade during his training.

Davis Rose did not like the term Jesus People. He said: "We're all God's children. We all belong to Jesus. I don't like the suggestion that the people in the Jesus Movement are in any kind of preferential position with him. Anybody who wants the Baptism can get it without identifying himself in any way with the Movement."

It was, most likely, this attitude that earned Davis Rose such wide acceptance in Kansas City from the start. He began by calling on leading pastors and assuring them that he had no intentions of emptying their churches. On the contrary, he was going to fill them. And he did just that. Rose had been in Kansas City eighteen months when I met him, and in that time his ministry had led over 10,000 young people to commit their lives to Christ, most of them receiving the Baptism. Rose also was a minister to older people; more than a thousand of them had made commitments.

Rose had strong feelings about parent-child relations. He said: "I caused my parents a lot of grief when I was a kid. I was selfish and self-centered, and I didn't think that I was getting my tenth of their love and attention. Now I can see that my folks loved all ten of us kids one hundred percent. The trouble was that I wasn't giving my love back. I've tried to teach the kids here in Kansas City that they can't be real Christians if they're having bad relations with their parents. Look at Jesus: he was still obeying his mother when he was a grown man. He didn't want to make the wine at the marriage feast at Cana, but he did it because Mary asked him to. I don't let any of the local kids stay at our communes unless it's okay with their parents."

A boy I met through Rose told me that he once hated his parents so much that he seriously plotted to kill them and came close to trying it several times. He said: "I got blamed for everything that went wrong in the house. Everybody was fighting all the time. It was awful. I ran away a few times, and I only went back because I was hungry. Then my friends started talking about Brother Dave's prayer meetings and I started going to them. One night I got the Baptism. Brother Dave let me stay in his house a few days, until I got used to what happened to me. Then

I had to go home and straighten things out. I told my parents that I loved them and that I wanted to be a good son. I told them that I had given my life to Jesus and that this was going to be the most important thing for me from then on. I did my chores around the house; I got back into school; I spent all my free time working for the Lord. It took a couple of months, but everything is all right at home now. My father doesn't understand about the Spirit, but we get along fine now and we really love each other. My mother has received the Baptism."

Because most of Rose's kids are locals, those who stayed at the dozen communes he had in cities and towns around Kansas City were either ex-addicts who benefited from the busy routines of communal life or kids whose parents had approved the idea. Rose's teams of traveling witnesses used the communes as stopovers. But the bulk of Rose's kids lived at home, went to school, held part-time jobs, and attended their own churches as well as Rose's Saturday night meetings at the spacious Second Presbyterian Church in a swanky part of town. Thus Davis Rose was not the same type of parent-stubstitute for his kids as, say, Tony and Susan Alamo were for theirs, and his work in Kansas City would not be as threatened by collapse upon the possibility of his departure.

This could be a good thing. Rose told me: "My wife and I are being called to Israel."

I asked: "By the Lord?"

"Yes. We have felt it for a long time."

"Have you any idea why?"

"Maybe he wants us to be there when he comes back."

"When do you think you'll go?"

"Whenever the Lord tells us."

Months later, I learned that David and Toni Rose would attend a gigantic witness-fest in Munich, Germany, in the summer of 1972, the fest sponsored by the Munich YMCA. That would put them halfway there.

The place was a mess. This was the last straw. He would have to close down.

For the year that Father Graham Pulkingham was pastor

of the Episcopal Church of the Redeemer in Houston, Texas, he had tried to involve the church in the community. This was no easy task. Gradually, the neighborhood had turned into a black and Mexican ghetto, and none of these people attended his church. For years, the church had had a thousand-member congregation, but as the neighborhood deteriorated, they became people who arrived and departed by car. When the priest who had been pastor for 25 years retired, it seemed that most of the congregation retired with him. When Father Pulkingham took over, there were so few parishioners that he was practically holding services for himself. This was why he wanted to become involved in the community. He hoped to draw on his neighbors to fill his church.

Adjacent to the church was a gymnasium that had been closed for years. Pulkingham opened it and invited the neighborhood kids to come in. They came in. What they didn't steal, they broke. Every night, Pulkingham faced a massive clean-up job, and he was going broke trying to replace the expensive equipment that had been damaged. It happened once too often. The priest got fed up. He closed down the place and he resigned himself to a pastorate of loneliness and boredom.

One day in a drugstore he saw a paperback book—*The Cross And The Switchblade*. He read the jacket copy. He bought the book and took it home. He read of how Dave Wilkerson had walked into the Brooklyn ghettos alone and brought teen-aged ganglords to Jesus. A few days later, Graham Pulkingham was in Brooklyn asking Dave Wilkerson how he did it. They consulted together for two days, when suddenly Wilkerson said: "The Lord had just spoken to me about you. Get on your knees. I want to pray over you." Pulkingham knelt; Wilkerson, touching him, prayed, and when Pulkingham got up he had the Baptism.

When Graham Pulkingham got back to Houston, things started happening fast. He didn't even have to go out after the neighborhood ganglords. They came to him, one or two at a time, and they would ask: "How come I'm always in trouble? How come every time I walk out of the house I get busted?"

And Pulkingham would say: "To answer that, I'll have to talk to you about the Lord."

"Go ahead."

Time and again, the kids would end up on their knees before leaving.

The neighborhood started changing again, for good. People began to hear about the effects of confiding in Father Pulkingham, and they went to him with all sorts of problems. Even when they held back some details from him, he could sense them and truly help. The gift of discernment. One Sunday morning, an amazing thing happened. The service had ended and people were leaving, and a woman tripped and fell and broke a leg, and her leg was bent where there was no joint. She was in great pain and people had to hold her down. Someone went for a doctor. Graham Pulkingham knelt beside her and prayed for her healing. She was healed, then and there. The gift of healing.

Something even more amazing happened. Four men came into Graham Pulkingham's life, and they were to change it. One man he already knew: Dr. Robert Eckert, a general practitioner in Hitchcock, Texas. When Pulkingham first told Eckert about what had happened to him at his church, the doctor was just amused. But he had a patient, a woman. whose worst illness was schizophrenia. She was always threatening to kill her children. After one particularly bad attack, Eckert sent the woman to Father Pulkingham, more in hope than in faith. The woman received the Baptism and she was cured. That cured Eckert of any doubts. He and his wife asked for and received the Baptism.

The second man already had the Baptism. He was Jerry Barker, a successful lawyer in Galveston. Barker's wife had developed an emotional illness and doctors said she would probably have to be institutionalized for the rest of her life. Barker was ready to go anywhere, do anything, spend everything for his wife's recovery. One night in 1964, while Barker was taking a walk, pondering his woes, he realized he had come to the end of his rope, and he said aloud: "All right, Lord, I'm turning this over to you. You'll have to cure Esther. I'll do anything you say, and

I won't do anything unless you tell me." The words were no sooner out of his mouth than Barker thought he was being mugged from behind. An explosion of joy blasted through him so forcefully that it hurt, and his legs buckled. When he came out of it, he saw that he was alone. Since he had just been talking to the Lord, he concluded that what had hit him was of the Lord. A religious man, active in the Episcopal church, he went home and spent a couple of hours doing detective work in his Bible. That was how he found out he had received the Baptism. Now he knew God would cure his wife, which He did.

Father Pulkingham had had the Baptism about a month when he met Barker, who'd had it about eighteen months. Talk about Pulkingham and his church was moving around in Episcopal circles and reached Barker, and he was sure he knew what had happened to the priest. He drove up to Houston, called on Pulkingham, and they shared.

The other two men were from Houston—Ladd Fields, an engineer, and John Grimmet, chief of a line crew for a power company. They had heard about Pulkingham, they were pretty sure what had happened to him, and they wanted it for themselves, so they went to him.

The four men met each other through Pulkingham, and they all became friends. Like Pulkingham, they were in their late thirties, married, and they all had children. They began meeting one morning a week at five o'clock at the church, to worship in the Spirit together. They began getting together in the evenings, as well, and before long they were getting together every evening. As the weeks passed, their wives and their children received the Spirit.

The idea struck them all at once: The Lord wanted them to live in community. And the Lord wanted them to live near the church. They obeyed the Lord. For Eckert and Barker, the obedience meant severe changes in life. Both had to give up lucrative practices and sell big houses. Ladd and Grimmet also had to get rid of their suburban homes. Their children transferred from the first-rate schools of the upper classes to the deprived schools of the inner city. Furthermore, all five men agreed that their community would not be for their own clique. Anybody who wanted to come in or needed to come in could come in, regardless of age, sex, race, creed or color.

These developments occurred in 1966 and 1967. On the day the Church of the Redeemer community began, there were four households. The first day, five people moved in with the Barkers, all of them black and two of them ill. By the middle of 1972, there were almost fifty communal households in the parish, occupied by about 300 people. With another 300 who lived elsewhere, these people comprised the core workers for what developed into a wide variety of parish projects and services. The parish has another 800 members who live elsewhere and take part in parish programs when they can.

Some of the programs were: a coffeehouse for young people; a shop for free clothes; a ranch for boys with home and/or drug problems; a jail ministry; a counseling program; a free medical clinic, headed by Dr. Eckert; a free legal advice office, headed by Barker; a bookstore; a literacy program; a medical ministry in Mexico; a traveling ministry, headed by Graham Pulkingham. The households operated on an open-door policy, day and night. All residents of the households pooled their incomes, with individual and family needs met as they came up. All of the residents either had the Baptism before they moved in or received it soon after. Most of the non-residents of the core group had the Baptism, as did many of the 800 who, for one reason or another, were not as active in the programs. Many of the residents and the congregation were young people. The average age was twenty-four. Over the past five or six years, many of the youngsters have gone into the ministry.

Jerry Barker said: "Nobody has a private life around here. We don't want any. What we do is serve. We serve the Lord by serving his children."

Jim Palosaari turned out to be the man I was looking for. As I traveled across the country, meeting Jesus kids in every town, I began to wonder how the whole thing was going to hold together, once its current superstars were gone. Jim Palosaari had wondered the same thing. Himself a superstar and probably the superstar who was making the greatest effort to keep the superstars in frequent touch with each other, he was more concerned about what shape the Jesus Movement would be in, say, twenty or thirty years from now than how many kids he had prayed into the Baptism yesterday.

"Of course," he said, "we're supposed to be in the End Times, so maybe I shouldn't worry about what's happening twenty or thirty years from now. But just in case there's anybody around then, I think it's time to get some organization into the Movement."

Jim Palosaari was trying to inject some organization by running a training school in Milwaukee and publishing *Street Level,* a Movement newspaper widely circulated in the Midwest. He told me: "I think the future strength of the Movement is here in the Midwest. California is full of transients. It always has been and it always will be. I know; I've lived there. Here in the Midwest, the current crop of transients is already in California. What we have left are more stable people. They're going to hang around. What they build will live. The Lord did the right thing by starting the Movement in California, with all the addicts. Those one-minute withdrawals got a lot of attention, and this brought other people into the Movement. Here it's different. I haven't had a single kid go through training who had been an addict. I wouldn't turn one down, of course. But these kids just didn't go that way. They're a different type, and I think they're the type of the future."

Palosaari was the only leader I met who had a good word for the Children of God. He said: "It's their training. It's terrific. Their kids are probably the best trained in the Movement. They know their Bible, they know leadership, they know organization. The only thing they don't know is love. They talk a lot about love, but what they function on is fear. The Children of God keep about ninety percent of the kids they recruit, but mostly because they tell them: 'If you leave us, you'll go straight to hell.' I would rather have a kid who loves souls and wants to do what he can to save them for Jesus."

Jim Palosaari was born in Oconomowoc, Wisconsin,

thirty miles west of Milwaukee. When he was younger, he wanted to be an actor, so he went to New York but he didn't have any luck and he gave up. He then went to California, not with hopes of getting into the movies, but because he decided to become a car salesman, and he knew everybody in California had to have at least two cars. He did very well, he made a lot of money, he got married and he had a couple of children.

But he wasn't happy. He knew that something was lacking in his life, but he couldn't figure out what it was. He just knew that he was unable to relate to anyone or anything. He started drinking heavily. He tried drugs. He fooled around. And yet that emptiness persisted; the discontent nagged at him. Finally he decided to chuck everything. He quit his job, he left his family, he took his money out of the bank, he bought a van, and he left town. For the next few years, he bummed up and down the West Coast and into Canada. Usually he had a girl with him.

In the summer of 1968, he was in the state of Washington. Daylight was ending, and he decided to find a place to spend the night. He took the next turn-off. He proceeded for several miles, and he came to a place called Maltby. Population: twenty-five. For no reason at all, he counted the graves in the cemetery as he passed it. Thirteen. Jumpy place. He passed a couple of stores and a few houses, and he was out of town. At the side of the road was a large tent, and on it was a sign: "Revival Tonight." Jim stopped the car. There didn't appear to be anything ahead except mountains, and he intended to turn around and go back to the main road with hopes of finding a livelier place to spend the night.

A young man came out of the tent and approached quickly, eying the van. He said: "Hi."

Jim said: "Hi."

"I'm Russ Griggs."

"Glad to know you."

Russ asked: "You people sleep in this thing?"

"Yeah."

"Some people here are letting us use their house. You can stay with us tonight."

Jim said: "We don't mind sleeping in here."

Griggs shrugged. "Suit yourself." He pointed. "Why don't you park it behind the tent? That way you won't get snarled in the traffic when all the people arrive."

Jim looked around. "*All* the people?"

"Yeah. Ranchers. The hills are full of 'em."

"I'm not sure we're staying."

Griggs said: "Oh. I thought you came for the meeting. Where are you from?"

"L.A. You?"

"We're from Vancouver. We're with the Jesus People Army."

"Jesus freaks?"

"If you want to call us that," said Griggs. "Brother, I've got to get ready for tonight. If you decide to stay, please park out back." And he returned to the tent.

Jim Palosaari looked around again. It was a pretty place. He shifted gears and pulled around to the back of the tent and parked. A truck was there and a couple of cars.

Later that evening, Jim heard a number of cars arrive. Gradually the conversation inside the tent grew to a small storm. Quiet, then, as a man spoke, but Jim couldn't quite make out what he was saying. Then came a great crash of guitars, drums, singing and handclapping. Jim said to his girlfriend: "Listen to them go at it." She nodded. They went at it for over an hour, and Jim found himself enjoying it. Then the man's voice again, again muffled, for almost an hour. Then more singing. In a little while, Jim could hear the talk and the laughter of the people as they left, calling good night to each other and saying they'd see each other tomorrow. And a little while after that, Russ Griggs and several other young people, some of them carrying musical instruments, came into sight and they went to the vehicles.

Palosaari was just a few feet away. He said: "Sounds like you people had a good time in there tonight."

Russ Griggs said: "Oh, yes. It's always a joy to praise the Lord. If you're around tomorrow night, why don't you join us?"

"Maybe we will."

Next evening, Jim and his girlfriend were in the tent, in the last row of folding chairs. It was terrific. As the people sang and clapped, some of them danced in the aisles, others shook hands and embraced. Griggs' sermon was long, but it was interesting, even though Jim Palosaari often got lost in the many Bible citations. More singing. Then the altar call. Jim was touched as he watched this person and that step into the aisle and go forward determinedly to make their commitment to the Lord. He wondered what they got out of it, what the kick was. Then more singing, and it was over.

Jim and his girlfriend were there the next night, and the next. On the next night, the last night of the revival, Russ Griggs changed the altar call. He asked everybody to stand. Then he said: "Brothers and sisters, I have a question I'm going to ask you. I'm going to ask you a question, and I want to hear your answer loud and clear. Loud and clear, brothers and sisters. Here's the question. Do you believe that Jesus Christ is your Lord and Savior? Let's hear your answer." There was a roaring yes. "Let me hear that again," Griggs said. Again the roar. Griggs said: "Good. Now, brothers and sisters, I want you to do something. All of you that said yes, all of you that said Jesus Christ is your Lord and Savior, I want you to come forward. Please come forward and line up here in front of the stage. All of you who said yes."

They began to go forward, row after row of seats emptying, until all of them were lined up in front of the stage. Except Jim and his girl. As the group formed, Griggs kept saying: "Praise Jesus. Praise the Lord. Bless us, Jesus." Jim was beginning to feel foolish. Griggs said: "This is beautiful, brothers and sisters. I know the Lord is happy to see all of you up here, witnessing for him. This is beautiful. Now, brothers and sisters, I want you all to turn around. Please turn around and face the back of the tent." They turned. Jim felt over a hundred pairs of eyes on him. He became uncomfortable.

Griggs said: "Now, brothers and sisters, you see that young couple back there? They're nice people. They've been visiting with us all week and coming to the services to share with us. But they don't know the Lord yet. They haven't met him. They didn't say yes when I asked the question and they didn't come forward. Well, I know that the Lord knows them and loves them and wants to enter their lives. Let's pray for them, brothers and sisters. Let's pray that the Lord won't wait to be invited into their lives. Let's pray that the Lord will enter their hearts on his own. Let's pray that the Lord will take them into his arms and bless them in the Spirit. Pray, brothers and sisters. Please pray."

Jim was embarrassed, annoyed, and he was starting to get angry. This was a rotten trick for Russ to pull. They had hardly discussed religion at all during their few minutes together every day as the group arrived and departed. Russ had no right to do this. Jim tried to take a step to leave, but he was startled to find himself immobile. What's all this? He did not want to look at the people down front, praying for him, some with their heads bowed, but many staring at him. He could not even understand what they were saying. He closed his eyes and bowed his head to shut them out. He became aware that his hands were shaking, and he looked at them. Fury? Fear? His arms began to shake. He looked at his girl. She had dropped to her knees, her face buried in her hands, and she was sobbing. Now Jim's shoulders were shaking, his abdomen, his whole body. What is this? Is there an earthquake? Is this death? Jim lost his balance and fell to the ground. When he tried to get up, he could rise only to his knees. He was frightened. He raised his arms and he moaned: "Oh, Jesus!" A great ecstasy filled him. . . .

They sat up half the night, the Jesus People explaining to Jim and Sue what had happened to them, that they had received the Baptism in the Holy Spirit, that their lives had been changed and they would never be the same. Jim asked: "Okay, but what do we do now? How do we live with the Baptism? What comes next?"

Russ asked: "Do you have any special plans?"

"No."

"Then why don't you stay with us? We're going back

to Vancouver and then we're going into Seattle. You can meet Linda Meissner."

"Who's she?"

"Our leader."

"A woman?"

"Yes. Wait 'til you meet her."

Within a week after Jim Palosaari met Linda Meissner, he was her chief aide.

I asked Palosaari what he thought of Linda, and he said: "She is a wonderful woman, a great leader, and a true Christian."

I asked: "What do you think about her joining the Children of God?"

"I can't understand it," he said. "That's not like Linda. She must have had her reasons. Maybe the Lord told her to do it. The Children better get ready for some changes."

"In what way?"

"Linda doesn't get along too well with women," he said. "She loves them in the Lord, of course, but she gets along better with men and she prefers to work with me. The Children of God are run by the two Berg sisters. I don't see Linda taking orders from them. It might end up the other way around."

It might.

One of the first big changes in Jim Palosaari's new life was that he obtained legal evidence from Los Angeles to show that his wife had divorced him, and this freed him to marry Sue.

Palosaari worked with Linda Meissner for about a year, when he perceived that the Lord wanted him to transfer his ministry to the Midwest. Though there was good Christian leadership in the bigger cities, groups of Jesus kids were forming in scores of towns in every state, and these were the kids who had to be reached and probably trained, Jim felt. Linda didn't want him to go, but she knew she shouldn't try to stop him. In fact, when he was starting out and needed some big names to help him attract crowds and get publicity, Linda made two trips to the Midwest to attend his rallies.

Jim considered settling in Chicago but, he said: "The

Lord opened up Milwaukee for us. Even before we did any serious looking for a place to live, the Lord led a man to us who had two big adjacent houses in Milwaukee, and that was too clear a sign for us to settle anywhere else."

Jim Palosaari's leadership program was like on-the-job training. The kids would undergo several weeks of intensive studies in Milwaukee. Then Jim would pick a destination for a group, give them a van and just enough money to get there and stay for a couple of weeks, and then they had to depend on the Lord to provide for them while there and on their way back, as they witnessed and rapped with the locals along the way. The returning groups then attended seminars, sharing their experiences, identifying their weak points, and resuming their studies for several more weeks before heading out again. When Jim felt a kid or a group of kids was ready, he would assign them to a smaller city or town, either to organize the Jesus kids or join those already there and assure them trained direction. Through this system, Palosaari was confident that he could turn out, year after year, a cadre of solid young Christians who, with the help of the Holy Spirit, would keep the Jesus Movement active, strong and growing, without the threat of cults, either in terms of personalities or theology, and without the danger of decrescence through stagnation.

Jim Palosaari had an unusual attitude toward the appearance of most Jesus People. His own hair was full but not long, he had a small beard, and when we met he was lounging around his office in a long robe. He said: "We don't need all these things, you know. I'm keeping mine until I can do enough missionary work. I tell the kids that they let their hair grow and grew beards and dressed like hippies because they wanted to identify themselves as protestors against the Establishment. These things were just protest symbols. I tell the kids that after they receive the Baptism and become true Christians, they don't need the symbols anymore because they aren't protesting in the same way. Frankly, I think the Movement would be growing even faster if we didn't look so funny. Anyway, I tell the kids the song doesn't say that they will know we are Christians by our long hair and beards and hippie clothes. The song says that they will know we are Christians by our love."

Scott Ross was a top New York disk jockey. He was buddies with the Beatles and the Rolling Stones, and they made time to be on his show when they were in town, keeping Ross high on the ratings. Other buddies kept Ross high on drugs, liquor and women. It was great to be young and rich and famous, even though half the time you didn't know what was going on. There were days when Ross couldn't remember a word he had said on his show. There were nights when he drew a total blank. There were mornings when he awoke in bed with total strangers. Then came the moment when he realized that his only means of survival was total surrender to somebody who would take over his life totally. He turned to Jesus.

And he turned away from all his old buddies. Radio was the only kind of work Scott Ross knew. He realized that he would have to get out of New York if he wanted to stay clean. Just changing stations wouldn't make any difference. The same press agents, the same struggling performers, the same publicity hounds would follow him, eager to give him anything he might wish for a few minutes of his air-time. And it would be the same whether he went to Pittsburgh or Podunk or Walla Walla. No. The change would have to be more severe than that. If he was now living for the Lord, he would have to be working for the Lord.

He was able to acquire a license for an FM station at Ithaca, New York, a town surrounded by colleges, and he began what he called the Christian Broadcasting Network. It was a one-man, one-station network, but that was good enough for starters. The station featured rock, but Scott's chatter was all about Jesus and all that his guests wanted to discuss was Jesus. Scott had a telephone hook-up which allowed conversations from callers to go out on the air, and the conversations were about Jesus.

Ross married. He and his wife lived in a mobile home. One morning in the early winter of 1969, they awoke to find that sub-zero temperatures had caused the water pipes in the kitchen to break, and the room was three inches under water. They would have to move.

On the air that day, Ross told people what had happened, and he said: "If any of you have any idea where we can live, give us a call here at the station and let's talk about it."

At that moment, a middle-aged widow was listening to Scott Ross for the first time. She was Peggy Hardesty, and she lived on a farm at Freeville, just outside Ithaca. She never listened to FM, but the AM section of her radio had gone on the fritz that day and now she had no choice. She tuned in Ross without really making a choice about it. When she heard him tell of his need for a home, she jotted down the telephone number he gave, and she called him.

She told him who she was and where she was located, and she said: "I've got a barn out here that you can use."

Ross said: "A barn?"

"Yes," she said. "It's very nice, and I won't charge you anything. I don't suppose you'd be staying there long, until you find a house or something, but it should do. I mean, if you're as desperate as you sound, we can fix it up."

"I'm desperate, Mrs. Hardesty," Ross said, "but I wasn't thinking about a barn. Can I come out and look at it?"

"Yes, of course. Any time."

He went out the next day. It was a nice barn, all right, but it was full of animals and it stank of manure. Ross was sure he had flipped just for making the trip. He thanked Peggy Hardesty and went back to town. His wife and their baby went to stay with relatives in Manhattan. Scott moved into a hotel while he hunted around for a new home.

He couldn't get that barn off his mind. One day he rented a plane and flew over the area. It sure was a nice barn. And the countryside was beautiful. The thought struck him: The barn should be a place of worship: The Gospel should be preached there. He put the idea out of his mind, but it kept coming back, like a gnat in summer.

Ross asked aloud: "Lord, is that you or is it just my head?"

A few days later he found himself walking up the driveway at the Hardesty farm, and when Peggy Hardesty saw him, she asked: "Well, Mr. Ross, have you decided to move in?"

"No, ma'am," he said. "I think I've got a place in town; I'll know tonight. But may I take another look at the barn, anyway?"

"Of course," she said. "And, Mr. Ross, if you don't want to live there, you can use the barn for anything else you want."

Scott Ross went into the barn alone and stood, looking around, unsure of himself and what was going on. He said: "All right, Lord, you show me." Guidance came in the form of an urge to clean out the place. Against one wall was a big stack of rotting wood. He began to carry it outside. Peggy Hardesty saw him and came over and asked: "What in the world are you doing?"

Ross asked: "Do you have any use for this wood, Mrs. Hardesty?"

"No," she said. "As a matter of fact, I've been meaning to get rid of it for years."

"Good. I'll send somebody out this afternoon to haul it away."

"May I ask what you're doing?"

"I wish I knew." And he went back into the barn for more wood.

When Ross returned to the farm the next morning, he located a shovel and a wheelbarrow and he went to work on the manure. He was not having much fun. He asked: "Lord, why are you having me do this?"

The answer: "Don't forget—this is where I was born."

Ross said: "Okay, Lord. No more questions."

And there were no more.

That day, when he went on the air, he said: "Let me tell you how I spent the morning. Or maybe you can smell it."

After that, every day, he reported on his progress at the barn. All he knew, he said, was that the Lord wanted him to turn it into a place of worship, and he invited: "If there is anybody out there who knows anything about building a cathedral, please come out to the barn and help me."

People came out. Students. Professors. Men in the building trades. Farmers. Lumbermen and plumbers and electricians provided their services and supplies. One day in March, it was as though the Lord had handed Scott Ross a blueprint, for suddenly Ross knew exactly what the Lord wanted. The barn was to become a combination of a place for prayer meetings, a coffeehouse, a training center, a retreat house and a crash pad for anybody who needed one. And that's what it became.

Ross named it the Love Inn.

That summer, so many kids were crashing at the Love Inn that Ross realized dormitories would have to be built, and they were. And the place was more than a flophouse. Some of the kids who arrived already had the Baptism; many more received it there. The kids held Bible classes. They took leadership courses. Groups went out as missionaries to other college towns. Campus-oriented FM stations elsewhere asked Ross for tapes of his broadcasts from the Love Inn, and thus the Christian Broadcasting Network actually became one. And not only did Peggy Hardesty deed the barn acreage to the Love Inn community, but she eventually deeded her entire thirty-acre farm to assure the kids a home, a growing home.

Scott Ross said to me: "It's a groove. All this, out of a barn. But that's where it all started, isn't it?"

9

Dig It!

(Following are a number of testimonies by the Jesus kids, of various ages, from various places, with various backgrounds. Some were told to me; others appeared in the Jesus People press; a few I have altered slightly, not so much for the sake of the kids as for their families.)

"About two years ago, I was walking around doing my own thing, smoking weed, getting busted on rides, trying to find my head on LSD. I had just moved out here from Oklahoma. All I knew about was booze and sex, until one day I met a couple of guys and turned on to a role of reds. I had just started high school. I was there about four weeks until one day in art class I crashed, and they took me to jail. Well, a year went by, in and out of jail.

"I started running around with some bikers, having a good time. My second year, I had to go to continuation school. Thought I was a real bad dude, trying to buy the world. But they taught me I wasn't as bad as I thought I was. So I got heavier into the LSD bag and played in a blues group. One day I found out I had three warrants for my arrest. So I split Hollywood and was living with some people I met there. One day I finally did it—got busted for possession while under the influence.

"Well, I had to do a little time. One day I was in the visiting room and I found a Jesus tract. I thought it was cool but not for me. I got out of camp, and one night I was really ticked off at my people for not letting me smoke dope in my room. So I headed to a partner's house. But on the way, there was this church. A lot of my friends were tripping out on going to church. At the time, I didn't even know why I wanted to go into that church—I just thought it would be a groove. But there was this cat, and he was telling me that I didn't really have peace, even on LSD. And that was true. So I said if this Jesus Christ can't give me more than what I've already got, then I'll shine the whole thing on. Praise the Lord, that guy was right. I said: 'Lord, do your thing in my life and give me that peace and joy that this cat told me about.' And he did. It's been two years now, and he hasn't let me down."

"Even as a little girl, my ambition in life was to be somebody, not so much in the society thing but in being recognized in love. The last two or three years were directed heavily toward that aim. Either I was going to be something special to the hip society or I was going to be recognized some day for all the dance knowledge I had. I didn't really think that I could ever have both, though I wanted both. During the day and evening, I instructed dancing; and after that, whatever happened was cool. I think the only moral I had—and that was only because my job was at stake—was not to go to bed with my students.

"People these days know that dope isn't where it's at, basically, or having a lot of money. All that man is trying to do is have a good time *now* because tomorrow might not come.

"This was where I was at: money if I wanted it, a guy, car, booze, dope, action, always something happening with somebody different. I didn't really believe there was any such thing as a lasting love because I'd never had anybody really love me through thick or thin.

"Having been raised in a Catholic background, I'd never heard anyone talk about Jesus so much as this Christian who approached me on the street one day. Only by the grace of God did I ever listen with my spiritual ear to what he had to say, because I was really soured on religion.

"Eleven months ago, Jesus set me free—from myself, from the world and from the hold of the devil. I just praise him today because of the work he's doing around the world and the light he's shining into my heart, changing me from gory to glory. That is my favorite promise from the Word. He's shown me that if I don't keep going up with him I will never be happy, and I could end up back on the old road downward. Also, the Lord has given me a husband. I pray that he'll teach me to love him better. I certainly can't love on my own strength."

"One Sunday morning I was eating breakfast when my brother came down the stairs like a bolt of lightning. He said: 'Nancy, I went to the Christian Coffeehouse last night, and I've got to tell you what I found out about Jesus.'

"He couldn't stop talking about Jesus and how important he is. He was so happy and his eyes just glowed, and I wanted this, too. So the next Saturday I went down to the coffeehouse with him to listen to the band, and the most beautiful thing happened. I was just listening to the words, and I got the strangest feeling inside of me. It was like I had just swallowed a big huge gulp of love and warmth. But at the same time I was afraid because Satan wanted me, too. So I talked to people who had already accepted Jesus into their lives. And soon Satan was cast out of my heart and love and understanding were in his place. Then I went home and started reading the Bible, which I had never even opened in my entire life.

"To understand everything better, I started going to Bible studies. Life is so beautiful now. My body is so full of love for everyone else around me. I have found everything I need through Christ. It's a beautiful feeling that everyone must find for themselves."

"My testimony with the Lord began when I was a very small boy. I really had a great love in my heart for Jesus but I lost it for many reasons. One reason was that I quit going to church because I never really felt any change at all when I came back from Sunday services. So I started doing the things I wanted to do with no regard for what Jesus wanted me to do. So I gradually pushed Jesus out of my life with my sins. So then I tried a lot of things to fill the gap I had created by pushing Jesus out of my life. I used drugs for three years. I started smoking pot and ended up using heroin. But this didn't fill the gap; it only widened.

"So a friend and I were down at the park one day smoking a joint and all of a sudden this cat comes up and starts rapping about how he used to use drugs, and he said the more he used the more frustrated and confused he got. And that now that he had accepted Jesus into his life all of this had gone away. So I read one of the Jesus People's papers and really started to understand where I had gone wrong in my relationship with Jesus. But still I wanted to have the Lord in my heart and still do what I wanted to do.

"So again I went on my way but this time I realized what I had to do to really have Jesus in my heart. So for a while I did go on my own way and I found myself getting back into my old ways. I even started to shoot dope again. One night I was just sitting there and I realized that I had to give up my life to Jesus. I did, and now that gap I used to have is completely gone since Jesus has come into my heart. The feeling is so great that you can't explain it. All

I can say is that you can have it, too, if you just give your whole self to him."

"I'm nineteen and am finally very happy. When I was a boy, I went to church a few times but gave it up because I couldn't understand what the guy in front was talking about. While I was there, though, I stole some money out of some purses that were down in the basement.

"All my life, all I've known is loneliness. My parents used to come home all the time, drunk and fighting. I used to lie awake at night, scared half to death, listening to them yelling at each other. One time my Mom was screaming for help and I went upstairs to see what was the matter, and my Dad had my Mom in a headlock and was choking her. I didn't know what to do; my Dad saw me and told me to get the hell downstairs. My parents never showed any love for themselves or us kids, and there were nine of us. My Dad worked all the time, and the only time I ever saw him was when he was beating on my mother or on Sunday when they would continue their bickering. I used to be scared to come home from school for fear that I would get spanked for something. School was a drag because I was always trying to get attention and so likewise never had any friends.

"When I got older, I would fight my Dad to protect my Mom because he would knock her around. The only time he tried to be a man was when he was drunk, and he thought that being a man was going around chopping up the furniture and my mother. My Dad finally had to quit his job because of drinking and not paying his bills. So for six years all he did was sit around and get drunk. We lived on welfare at this time, and I went out and did odd jobs so that the family could have a decent Christmas of booze and presents.

"As I got older, I would sneak out of the house and steal cars. I finally stole one and got in a wreck and got sent up. I've been in three juvenile institutions, all for long periods of time. In these institutions, I found out that I was a homosexual. I didn't know why it had to happen to me, but I liked boys. I did some experimenting with it in the institution and got busted for it. So all the guys went around calling me a fag and picking fights with me. I put up with this for eight months at that place. In this institution, psychiatrists, supervisors and me tried to change me from being what I was. It didn't work but only brought frustration and torment.

"I finally decided that I was a fag and I was going to have to live the life, and, brother, did I! I went to Seattle, where there are over 100 gay bars. I was seventeen and going to bars and drinking. I thought booze was the answer but it only made me more lonely. I turned on in Seattle to acid, weed and speed, and pushed it. I got bored with Seattle and came back home and I got arrested for possession. I spent sixty days in the clink and was found not guilty.

"A week later I went to San Francisco, home of the gay world. I was working in gay bars, as a waiter serving drinks and as a go-go dancer. All this time I found people wanted anything that could satisfy themselves, no matter if it hurt you or not. I got used and hurt so much that I had to do it back for my own protection, so I could survive. And in Frisco you have to be on your toes. I got more into speed, I was taking fifteen hits a day, steady for two years, besides dumping booze down me as much as I could get down. I had to get drunk or be on acid in order not to face the cruelty of this world. You think this world is groovy? Well, go to Frisco and be sure to take your flowers with you, along with a knife in case someone wants to take a poke at you.

"I had love affairs with guys, and they turned me into an alcoholic because I had to hide the hurt with booze. I was drunk continuously or wiped out on something. During my stay in California, I ran into some money and traveled all over the U. S., on first-class jets. I stayed in the most expensive hotels, ate the best food and drank the best booze. Money only made me more lonely.

"All my life there has been an emptiness inside, deep. I tried to fill it with booze, dope, sex and money. They didn't work but only made a mess out of me. I came back home in the hopes of getting myself together. It was the same thing here: booze, sex, emptiness, loneliness, and pain from past scars. I didn't care what happened to me. Finally I went out and stole a car. I got arrested and put in jail. With a record a mile long, I was facing twenty years. I got three months in jail and three years probation. Brother, that's a miracle! The state gave me a program: free school plus living expenses so I could get rehabilitated. I thought, wow! I can finally get myself together. But when I got out of jail it was the same thing—booze, dope, and loneliness.

"Five days later, a hippie with long scraggly hair, who didn't look worth anything, said to me on the street: 'God bless you.' That freaked me. I had never heard that before. But the clincher was that he meant it and showed love. He told me that Jesus loved me and wanted to give me love, happiness, peace and joy and that he even loved a faggot. And I believed him because I could see all these things in that kid's eyes and I could feel the love. That night Jesus came into my heart and poured so much love and happiness inside that I thought my heart would burst, but God's love kept pouring in and still is. The desire for speed and booze was taken away. And thanks to God, I no longer need to have sex with a guy or have that hunger for love because God's love is inside my heart. He has filled all needs. That love is beautiful. Jesus is far out."

"I'm nineteen, and I'm the daughter of a Nazarene minister. For fifteen years I believed in God, but I didn't really know Him. By 1967, I was disenchanted with life, and all I wanted to do was die. I tried to commit suicide but it didn't work.

"In my sophomore year, I got involved in ESP. In my junior year, astrology and horoscopes were my thing. All this time, I was trying to carry on a normal life in an imaginary world. Many times during my senior year I didn't know if things were real or imaginary.

"Then the Lord started showing me how much he really loved me. I started thinking about him more. Not long after that, as I was alone in my room, something really shook me. I started to sing in tongues and I realized I had received the Baptism in the Holy Spirit. I had my first personal encounter with God. The Lord helped me get through the suicidal trips and my fantasies, and cleaned all that trash out of my life.

Then I got an eye disease and my vision began to go and the doctors said I would go blind. But the Lord tested me. He asked me if I really believed he was a miracle-working God. When I said yes, I felt the healing power of God flow through my body. My eyes were cured. I was also cured of extremely bad nerves and low blood sugar. Thank you, Jesus."

"I was born and raised a Roman Catholic. I was educated in a Roman Catholic elementary school, Catholic high school, and a Catholic university. I studied out of Xavier University in New Orleans, Louisiana, as a math and physics major. I changed from math and physics to electronic engineering in Los Angeles, California. I worked in the field of electronics for approximately thirteen years, simultaneously becoming an alcoholic and a doper.

"I have been into something of every scene; I have seen a lot of it. I have handled a lot of it. I have been everything from a professional thug to a professional failure.

"I was in the black militant scene for a while. I was also in quite a few jails throughout the country. Jails from Lincoln Heights in Los Angeles, San Bruno in San Francisco to the Tombs in New York City, and practically every jail in every major city in-between. God started dealing with my life when I left the militant scene in 1969. I started going back and forth to San Bruno so much that, by October, I could no longer relate to jails—not in California or anywhere else—so I quit the scene with the intention of going to New York City.

"Instead I got as far as Salt Lake City. I was there a few months and took off for Wyoming—anywhere, for no special reason—just to get out of Utah. In Wyoming, some brothers stopped and picked me up and gave me a ride to Portland, Oregon. I had no reason to be in Portland, either. So I had a choice: I could either go back to San Francisco or up to Seattle.

"I took the alternate—I went to Seattle, and that's where

God got me. Of course, I didn't know this at that time. I'd been in Seattle for a few days; I went to a movie to see a documentary about Martin Luther King. I came out of the movie more uptight than ever, to be greeted by some hippie types passing out some flyers advertising a 'March For Christ.' I looked at the person that gave it to me, and I just said to myself and to my partner, 'Wow, these hippies, they got a brand new bag.' And we just walked away from that.

"But a few days later I was in downtown Seattle getting high and a couple of people approached me with Bibles in their hands. I saw them coming and right away my defenses went up. One of them said: 'Brother, can we talk to you?'

"I said: 'No.'

"So he said: 'Well, brother, can we talk to you later?'

"I said: 'Yeah. Later.'

"So they went away. But they came back later and they said: 'Brother, remember us?'

"Before I knew it, one of them had me by the arm, my booze still in one hand, and they led me to their car and they drove away with me. I didn't care—I couldn't have cared less—just a matter of relocating, because I knew that I could get just as high on one side of town as I could on the other.

"I arrived at the Seattle Center—at the arena they have there—and right away I saw that it was a revival. I sat there and I listened to them and the thing at that revival that caught my attention was the Roman Catholic priest that got up there to speak. I listened to him and after he finished speaking I went back and spoke to him awhile. Somehow, without my ever intending it, I answered the altar call later and I went right up there and got saved.

"And later that day I ended up at a Christian commune called the House of Joshua. Being as rebellious as I had been all my life, and with as much hatred as I had in my heart, it was kind of hard for me to really accept Jesus Christ. So I had to sit around and watch the Christians for awhile just to try and figure out what was happening because it really freaked me out. I sat around for three days afraid to eat anything because I was suspicious of that many people so happy all at the same time. I had just seen quite a few riots, I had seen quite a bit of rebellion throughout the world, and I had been prepared to do the next best thing. And when I finally realized the reality of Jesus Christ, I wanted all that I could get, all that he had to offer, I finally gave in.

"I thank him for choosing me because I didn't deserve to be his servant, having been so wrong all of my life. Something I haven't had is compassion, and I thank God for giving it to me."

"Most of my life has been hectic, confusing and unusual since early girlhood. I lived in many different places with many different kinds of religion. This all became so confusing. I wondered why people didn't love each other, why they weren't together. Why didn't religion help? Why, if everybody believed in God, they still rebuked one another on a denominational basis. It all seemed to lead to one place, to God, but people were fighting with each other to get there.

"Deep in my heart, I was searching for the truth about what God really was, wondering what is truth. I got strung out on drugs for four years in my search for spirituality and God. I wanted the truth so bad that I tried Eastern philosophy, witchcraft, astrology. All these things, they seemed to lead me from the truth further than ever.

"My Tarot cards couldn't bring me the love and happiness I was missing. Where was love, joy, peace and happiness? My mind was gone. I was in such darkness. I was crying out in pain. My mind was gone from drugs. My soul withered. My body was a physical wreck.

"Well, I was at Vortex, one of the festivals for dopers in Oregon, and a couple of times people came up to me with a glow of happiness that wasn't put on. I couldn't look at them straight. They stared right through me. It felt good, though. Then they told me of Jesus Christ. Before this, I had always said go away, out of my fear. But this time, I realized, I might try it. One last try for happiness.

"It worked! Hallelujah!

"When you accept Jesus Christ, he makes you free, happy and joyful. He raises you above the world, above fear, above hate, greed, above Satan. And he gives you love, joy, peace and harmony where it counts. On the inside. He healed my mind, my soul and my body by working in me with the Spirit of the Holy Ghost."

"I was born and raised in Wisconsin. My father owned a hardware store. We were a Jewish family; we observed the High Holy Days, but that was about all. I did pretty well in high school, and then I entered the University of Southern Illinois. My new friends turned me on to pot and acid and a few other things. Because of all the side activities, I had a rough time with my grades in college, and I was lucky to get my degree in chemistry.

"I went back to Wisconsin and I started teaching science in an elementary school. I could relate to the kids all right, but I didn't think I was achieving anything of value. I didn't feel I was doing anything that would have a lasting effect on anybody, and I soon got bored with the whole thing. I started to take a couple of joints to school everyday. When I felt like it, I'd tell the kids to write an essay about something and then go out in the schoolyard and turn on. I knew I wasn't going to stay with teaching long. As the school year ended, I bought a bike and got to know some bikers. That summer, we rode around the Midwest, crashing and swinging.

"I decided to give teaching one more year, but it was a bad year. Most evenings, I was out on my bike, getting into every scene I could. To keep from blowing my mind, I made a project out of some of the black kids at school, getting to know their families and trying to help them with their problems, but everything I tried to accomplish was blocked by red tape and prejudice. At the end of the year, I didn't tell anybody that I had quit teaching, but I knew I had.

"A buddy and I rode our bikes out to California, crashing around. We were in California about a week, then headed back. At the end of the day, I noticed a hippie commune up ahead. We went in there and asked if we could crash, and they said yes. The first odd thing I noticed was that everybody was busy. Nobody was lying around stoned. Those who weren't working were rapping in small groups, intently, thick black books on their laps. I didn't get the message until we all sat down for supper. One guy asked for a blessing on the food, and he said the name of Jesus. So they were Jesus Freaks.

"My buddy wanted to take off, but I was interested in finding out how Jesus Freaks spent the evening. They spent the evening at Bible studies and a prayer meeting. I was curious, so I sat in on a Bible class and I attended the prayer meeting. Everybody seemed so happy. They kept talking about loving one another in the Lord. And they were always praising Jesus. As a stranger and as a Jew, I was emotionally prepared to feel like an outsider; but they kept bringing me into their conversations, they kept shaking hands with me, giving me the grip; and during the hymns, anybody who noticed I wasn't singing came over to me with a hymnal, and then put an arm around my shoulders as we shared the book and I faked my way through the song. I was having a good time without knowing what it was all about.

"In the morning when I got up around eight, I found out that the kids in the commune had been up for three hours and were already at their studies and chores. A girl fixed breakfast for my buddy and me and then gave us some sandwiches for the road, and when we left her, she said: 'We'll all be praying for you.' I thanked her. We found the elder. He wouldn't take any money for the crash, so I thanked him and we said good-bye and shook the grip, and he said: 'Remember, brother, Jesus loves you.' I said yeah.

"We left. We were on the road about two hours, and I couldn't stop thinking about those kids. I had never met so many happy people at one time in my life. They were so dedicated; their lives seemed to have such purpose. I didn't know what it was they had, but I knew I wanted it for myself, and if it was Jesus, then I wanted him, too.

"Finally I knew I had to go back. I signalled my buddy that I was stopping, and when he got up to me I said: 'I'm going back to the commune.'

"He said: 'You forgot something?'

"I said: 'No. I'm just going back.'

" 'For how long?'

" 'I don't know. Maybe forever.'

" 'You're crazy.'

" 'Maybe.'

"He got angry. 'You little bastard,' he said, 'are you gonna let me make the trip all the way back to Wisconsin alone?'

"I gunned my bike, getting ready for the turn. I said: 'I'm sorry.' He raised his fist at me and called me some more dirty names. I made the turn. I headed back. They weren't surprised to see me.

"The Lord gave me the Baptism that first night. Right away, I spoke in tongues. Later, I found that I could also interpret. And, I believe, I was given the gift of knowledge. There's no other explanation for how I learned my Bible so fast. I stayed at the commune almost three months. Then the Lord told me that he wanted me to work among the Jews. I told the elder this, and he told me about Brother Moishe Rosen and the Jews For Jesus at San Francisco. I wrote him; he asked me to come and see him, and I did. He arranged for me to enter a Bible college near his place, and after I'm ordained I'll be doing the same kind of work he does.

"Before entering the college, I went back to Wisconsin to get my things. I had already written my family about what had happened to me. They didn't mind too much, except when I tried to evangelize them. My father couldn't understand how I could so easily abandon my Jewish culture. I told him I hadn't abandoned it, that I was more Jewish than ever, even more Jewish than he. I had simply done what the prophets had said I should do. I accepted Jesus Christ as the Messiah. I became a completed Jew.

"I am in Bible college now. I street-witness every night. I am going to get married. My parents should like her. She is a nice Jewish girl—completed."

"For years the Lord has been drawing me along. I think I've always tried to be a good Catholic. For the longest time, though, that meant that I had to *do* this and that in order to really 'make it.' It was a matter of always going to Mass on Sunday, of saying 'Good morning, Father' as I walked past the smiling priest at the church door. It was giving to this collection or to that collection. It was saying memorized or mechanized prayers.

"Then my faith wasn't in Jesus himself. He wasn't a person, and he wasn't that living for me. Sometimes I would question whether a God existed at all. I continued to try to live a good life. I kept all the rules. But it was a bland existence. I wasn't alive. I knew no personal Savior. He was an abstraction or historical figure of two thousand years past in my mind. In all of this, the Lord's Spirit was moving me along, deepening my awareness, gradually pricking my conscience, challenging me within, questioning. I worked in the business world while I was in high school. What I saw dissatisfied me very much. Was this what I wanted to do all my life? Was it money I wanted? It certainly didn't seem to be making the people around me any happier.

"The city of San Francisco was harsh. I grew up in the Fillmore District there, which is a black ghetto known all over California, and every bit as vicious as Watts in Los Angeles or Harlem in New York. In this situation I simply had to turn to someone for help. With as much faith as I could muster, I asked God to lead me where He wanted me to go. All of my life was spent in Catholic schools, and for this I am grateful, for I did meet the Lord there, too, occasionally. If it wasn't for those little prayer warriors and the Jesuit priests and scholastics I wouldn't be where I am today. Of this I am positive!

"I felt within me a desire to serve God with my whole life. I wanted to go all the way. All through high school I thought of being a priest. This was a way of giving my life. I entered the Society of Jesus, for it seemed the most obvious step to take at the time. I have loved every moment since, for it has been within the Jesuits that an even more intense awakening in me took place. The structure and order and necessary disicpline in such an organization are nothing compared to the tremendous ability to be with

Jesus totally and to share companionship with others of similar vision. But again, the Spirit led me from the desert to the mountaintop.

"In the summer of 1970, before I came to Gonzaga University, Spokane, I was at the University of San Francisco for summer school. It was here that I first became acquainted with the charismatic movement that was sweeping the Catholic Church throughout the United States. I went to a few prayer meetings and was greatly impressed by them. When I came to Spokane, I became familiar with prayer groups at Fort Wright College through a Jesuit brother of mine. Meanwhile, I read a great deal more about the movement and about the Baptism in the Holy Spirit. I discerned the Spirit of Christ here. After discussing this with my Spiritual Director (every Jesuit usually chooses an older Jesuit priest to help discern the Spirit in his life), I decided to ask the Lord for this Baptism, which for me was only a deepening of the Life I already felt within me. I prayed for the fruits of the Spirit: Faith, Hope, Love, Peace and Joy. Whatever else the Lord wished to give me, I'd also gladly accept. For me, the Baptism in the Holy Spirit was a more public commitment of the commitment I had already made to Jesus. That night I received this Baptism. No walls crumbled around me, no winds blew (maybe a sneeze or two), no clouds opened up; I heard no voices outside of those praying around me, and I didn't begin to speak in tongues. I can only vividly remember a tremendous deepening of my love for Jesus suddenly alive in my life, and a desire to serve him more fully as a priest in his Society and in his church. I also felt so happy that I wanted to sing a song. I tried to, but forgot the words.

"Since then, I've felt like a house on fire, excited with the Spirit of God within me. I have never before felt so much enthusiasm for a person in my whole life!"

"Getting on a bus one night, feeling like I wanted to end it all—all the way out—I heard a man let go of a four-letter word as he threw down a paper. I picked it up, the Hollywood Free Paper. Seeing what it was, I folded it and put it in my pocket. After getting home around one a.m., I read the paper.

"That made me feel a little better. Then seeing a phone number, I called—by that time it was three a.m., and a very drowsy voice answered.

"I began to unload over the phone. After we talked for awhile, I thought: here is a friend, someone who understands me. I, who had been through the wringer—addict, alcoholic, strung out. Everything there is to be had, I've had it! And here is a man who understands me. Wow! We prayed over the phone, and I was to call back the next day.

"I didn't wake until one that afternoon, but since then I've been alive with a renewed spirit. Jesus is so real, so near to me, and the Holy Spirit so beautiful. The friends at the HFP have become my family. It's home, and I'm at peace with God and myself."

"Most of the testimonies you hear from other girls show evidence of a beautiful change that has been completed by our Lord. Although my testimony doesn't appear on the outside to be a significant change, it is true that I, like everyone else, needed the love of our Father so badly.

"According to man's law, I never really did anything wrong. I stayed nicely within the demands of society by being a social freak. It is hard to explain just how much of a bummer it is not to be able to talk to someone because he isn't as good-looking as the people I was used to going around with. And it wasn't only looks, but it was the whole trip of having to know certain people because they were supposed to be cool.

"A society freak is so hemmed in by all of the ties that bind him to his ego. Ego separates man from man but, much more importantly, ego separates man from Jesus. And my Jesus freed me from the jail that I had built for myself. By looking at people and knowing that Jesus does love them, Jesus is letting me see them as people, with real feelings, real bummers, real joys, and he is opening me up to them.

"This is what Jesus has given me: a freedom from myself as I learn to yield to him and, because of Jesus' perfect love, the freedom to love everyone."

10

Quo Vadis?

It is impossible to generalize about the Jesus People, young or old, Protestant, Catholic or Jew. Moreover, it is impossible to appraise the Jesus Movement itself only on a basis of one's own spiritual experiences. In twenty years with *Guideposts Magazine,* I have interviewed hundreds of people about events in their lives that were of a spiritual nature. I can't read minds and I don't think I have the gift of discernment; but after several years at this, one does develop a certain perception, one does acquire an ability to listen between the lines, one learns to empathize without being carried away. Furthermore, with the Jesus People, besides my interviews, I collected about thirty pounds of printed matter—newsletters, newspapers, magazines, books—and I read them all and tried to understand them before I sat down to this report. I also had available to me the extensive file compiled by the *Guideposts* staff. I had John and Tibby Sherrill with whom I could compare reactions to certain people and events. And I had my own convictions. I had, as well, my professional obligations to report as accurately as I could without prejudice, to reflect without trying to persuade. Despite the fact that I have published many thousands of words on religious matters, I am not a professional religionist. I have also published many thousands of words on other matters, for I am a professional journalist. I decided to inject myself into this book, something I have never done before, simply because I felt this would provide a continuity in an account which otherwise might have become too episodic.

I knew from the start that the Jesus People had their critics. They were accused of being faddists. They were accused of being naive. They were accused of being emotional. They were accused of being poorly educated scholastically and poorly trained in religion. They were accused of being indifferent to the social problems of today's world. They were accused of using religion as a drug substitute. They were accused of blasphemy. They were accused of heresy. They were accused of mental instability. They were accused of dropping out on life.

I found that some of this was true about some of the Jesus People, but not all of it was true about all of them, and most of it wasn't true about any of them. I found that, too often, judgments were being made on the basis of the exterior appearance and behavior of the Jesus People rather than on the interior changes in their lives. I found that, too often, judgments of the entire nationwide Jesus Movement were based on visits to three or four of the better-known California groups. Appraisals of the Movement were being made without any acknowledgment of the Jewish and Catholic wings. Too often, I found, the Jesus People were being criticized not because they were wrong but because they were different.

I visited dozens of groups, interviewed their leaders, plus hundreds of Jesus People of all ages and all denominational persuasions. Some said they didn't want any publicity, which is why I have not mentioned them. Even so, I knew I was just skimming the surface. There was so much more to the Movement that I was unable to see because I had only two months for travel. I'd heard about a group in Louisville, Kentucky, that was having an incredibly healing ministry. I wanted to meet Episcopal Father Dennis Bennett who received the Baptism several years ago while rector of St. Mark's in Van Nuys, California. His enthusiasm for the Spirit did not go over well with many of his parishioners, and the pressure forced him to resign. He was given a run-down parish in Olympia, Washington, where Bishop William Fisher Lewis allowed him to evangelize in the Spirit. The Bishop later said: "It was the worst parish in the diocese when Father Dennis took it, and now it is the best." I wanted to meet Reverend Harold Bredesen, pastor of the First Reformed Church in Mount Vernon, New York. Pastor Bredesen was directly responsible for the Holy Spirit revival at Yale in 1964, after accepting an invitation from a number of students to spend an evening there explaining to them what the Baptism in the Holy Spirit was. Pastor Bredesen was also the first person John Sherrill interviewed as he began work on the book which led to his own Baptism.

I especially wanted to visit Asbury College, at Wilmore, Kentucky, where, in February, 1970, an ordinary morning chapel service erupted into a Holy Spirit revival which swept across the campus and, in a week, swept to campuses across the country. *Guideposts* published an article on Asbury in the December, 1971, issue, and it brought the following letter from a young man who had been a student at Asbury at the time but was now in the military:

"After having read your last issue and the story on *The Surging Spirit,* I thought: 'The next one just has to be about

Asbury.' That statement was half-fact, half-hope, all prayer. I'd waited a long time to read about the school—a school where God saw fit to walk through and change, where God sometimes pointed out directions, gave gentle shoves, and, in some cases, delivered a whop in the seat of the pants and got people moving, moving out in all directions. From my seat in the junior section of that very special chapel, it was impossible to see to what lengths God would go to get His people to listen to Him. We gathered one evening in the dorm to watch a nationwide TV news broadcast on the rumor that they had picked up the news about the revival. Instead they showed the heated arguments over a wage dispute of some kind. It seemed as though somebody just slugged us in the stomachs and laughed as we struggled with the idea that maybe the world doesn't want to know that some teen-agers aren't bad. Some teens love people. Some teens love God, and that even some adults have enough sense to ask God for help and forgiveness and a new start, even if it's embarrassing—since so many of their own students had thought them already to be in God's grace. There were reports that parents sent back clippings from Page 4 of this newspaper or that. The thing is, when God walked through our campus, He didn't leave us behind. One of the biggest fires He got started was the burning urge to introduce our traveling companion to other people. And if these other people have never read about what happened at Asbury, how are they ever going to know unless we speak up?"

That sounded like a good kid to me, and I thought about him when I considered the criticisms directed at the Jesus People. Dr. Lowell D. Streiker, a completed Jew, who teaches religion courses at Temple University in Philadelphia, visited a few of the California groups, and he later published an account of his trip. I was surprised by how greatly our reactions to the same people and situations differed. Dr. Streiker admitted that he was reduced to tears by the thought of the damage the Jesus People were doing to Christianity. He said that the fact that the Movement had provided the means for tens of thousands of kids to kick their drug habits did not justify the damage, assuming that the kids were permanently cured. And, in italics, he declared that the saddest thing he had to say about the whole thing was that the newly enfranchised kids probably wouldn't vote in the 1972 Presidential election because they cared so little about their country and the world.

Okay. I couldn't figure out how it could be determined whether the Jesus kids voted in the election or how they voted. But I was sure that if the issue of prayers in public schools were on the ballot, Tony and Susan Alamo would lead the parade of their kids to the polls. I thought, too, about the two members of the Christian World Liberation Front who had campaigned and won election to the Berkeley student government. I was sure that if they hadn't cared they wouldn't have bothered. As for the damages, the only bruise inflicted upon Christianity which seemed to me to be worse than the Protestant Reformation was the Council of Trent that followed it. The first unleashed personal interpretation of the faith into a maelstrom of disunity and the second put such a harness on it that the only Catholics allowed any personal opinions were the popes. These two events spewed such hatred in the world that five hundred years had to pass before Protestants and Catholics could worship together as Christians, through the Jesus Movement, in the Spirit.

On January 17, 1972, Harriet Van Horne, whom I admire, devoted her column in the New York Post to the Jesus Movement. I once read an article about Harriet Van Horne in which she said that she did not do much actual legwork but gathered most of the material for her columns through extensive reading. This column appeared to be based mostly on an article in *Trans-Action,* by Robert L. Adams and Robert Jon Fox. Miss Van Horne quoted the article as saying: "Members of the Jesus Movement have a high incidence of past drug use. . . ."

I thought: "That's right, and thank God it's *past* use." Miss Van Horne commented:

"Most disturbing parallel of all, the 'Jesus high' is being compared to a drug high. This is a perversion of religion, even though one may sincerely hope that coming to Jesus will render the drug high obsolete.

"There are all varieties of religious experience but it is still somewhat startling to read that a common description of coming to Jesus is: 'It's a rush like speed.' "

I knew this was true, too. It took me a couple of weeks to get used to listening to spiritual experiences in these terms, especially when they came out of such educated men as Don Williams and Jack Sparks. But these men worked with kids, so they had to speak the language of kids; and if the drug jargon was the only leftover the kids had from their drug scenes, then, again, thank God. In Spokane, Carl Parks told me: "I often find it effective to teach a Bible class in terms of sex. The kids understand sex. I use the drug lingo with them, too, of course. They understand that. And that's been the whole problem with kids, getting through to them. Can you imagine how far I'd get with the kids if I just threw King James at them without breaking it down?" I could imagine. Later, when I compared Jack Sparks' translations of the Epistles to every Bible I had in the house, I found Sparks' *Letters to Street Christians* by far the most lucid and explicit. But I realized that perhaps I had been over-exposed to the stuff.

Which reminds me of a lesson I learned on the trip, something I had no intention of using until now. I had stopped off at Palo Alto to meet Lambert Dolphin. Dolphin had been a highly successful physicist when he experienced the Baptism, and he decided to put his career aside in order to evangelize college campuses all over the world, in conjection with Campus Crusade. Dolphin had a rambling, Spanish-type house several miles out of town. Staying with him were seven or eight young men, all in the Baptism, who were in the process of completing their high school and college educations.

Lambert Dolphin was on the road when I called at his home unexpectedly one afternoon; but three or four of the young men were there, and they invited me in to relax a while before continuing on to San Francisco. We talked; I heard their testimonies, similar to others I'd heard elsewhere. I noticed that one young man was smoking cigarettes as we talked, and I awaited a propitious moment to question him about that. The afternoon was hot and muggy.

This young man volunteered: "I'll see if there's anything cold to drink in the refrigerator." He was back in a moment with a bottle of wine, and he said: "There's just this. We were chilling it for dinner tonight."

I asked: "You people drink wine with dinner?"

He gave me a look that also gave me a label. He said: "Yeah, we drink wine with dinner. So did Jesus. He even made the stuff." He saw my glance at his cigarette, and he said: "Jesus didn't smoke cigarettes because they didn't have them in his day." He appeared to make a decision, and he said:

"Listen, I want to tell you something. Several months ago, the guys decided that it would be nice to have a sauna bath around here. We asked Lambert and he said yes, so we built one ourselves. It's great. Well, Lambert knows a lot of people; they're always coming out here unexpected, like you. We're used to it.

"One afternoon, a couple of months ago, two of the guys were in the sauna. I was sitting here, studying. Somebody knocked on the door, and I went to answer it. They were some of Lambert's friends from town, five or six of them, men and women. I told them that Lambert was away but that they could come in and look around if they wanted. They came in and looked around and then we sat here, talking. I forget completely about the two guys in the sauna. They didn't know we had company. So they came out of the sauna without any clothes on and came into the house on the way to their rooms, and they walked right in on us. The women yiped and howled. The two guys ducked out of sight. And I went to their rooms to get clothes to take to them. They got dressed and they came in and apologized. We all had a good laugh and forgot about it.

"Lambert came home about two weeks later, and one night he had dinner with friends in town. When he got home that night, he was really uptight and wanted to know what was going on. He said his friends had told him they had heard that Lambert was running a place out here for homosexuals who were walking around naked all the time."

He stopped. He looked at me, waiting.

I said: "I get your point." It was a point I tried to keep

in mind on the rest of the trip and during the writing of this book. One must be cautious when making judgments which affect the lives of others, especially when one can't read minds.

Harriet Van Horne ended her column with the question: "What will happen to these young people when they are no longer high on Jesus?"

Who knows?

I have two friends who are qualified to speak in this area. One is Richard Gilmore, supervisor of the drug rehabilitation program in Washtenaw County, Michigan, at Ann Arbor. Previously, Gilmore established himself in work with young addicts at Project ReHab in Grand Rapids, where the rate of teen-age addiction was going down while it was rising everywhere else in the country. Dick Gilmore is himself an ex-addict, getting on to morphine pills during his boyhood in Brooklyn, a boyhood that would have qualified him for a role in *The Cross and the Switchblade*. But Gilmore was always a religion-oriented boy; he attended seminaries between his relapses into drugs, and he has been licensed to preach by his church. Dick Gilmore, a black man who never knew his father, kicked drugs in 1967, when the minister who had tried to guide him most of his life lost patience after another relapse and said: "Dick, I don't know what I'm going to do with you. If I didn't love you, I'd throw you out of my life." That did it. Somebody loved him.

Gilmore told me: "The Jesus trip works only with addicts who are already Jesus-oriented, regardless of how long ago the experience was or how brief it was. Substitute drugs and psychiatry are important supportive therapies, but even they won't work unless there is a crucial ingredient present—love, a stubborn, gripping love that can withstand extreme frustrations and repeated disappointments. I let the doctors give the kids the drugs and the psychotherapy. I give them love. Now, if young addicts find out that Jesus loves them more than everybody else in the world can, that could do it, but my experience has been that there has to be some orientation in that direction, no matter how slim and remote."

The other friend is Dr. Pasquale A. Carone, medical director of the South Oaks Hospital, Amityville, New York, one of the largest privately-operated psychiatric hospitals in the country. Dr. Carone is also the consulting psychiatrist to a major Catholic seminary in the East, where a couple of hundred young men take their final studies before ordination. Dr. Carone told me: "At the present time, there are twelve young men in the seminary who speak in tongues. I have been working with all of them for years. Six of them have histories of schizophrenia, and so I have to take into account the possibility that they may be hallucinating when they speak in tongues. But the other six are entirely free of symptoms of any disorders so I have to accept them as being sincere and expressing a valid spiritual experience."

Just as the Catholic Pentecostals told me how grateful they were to the Protestants in the Jesus Movement for revitalizing the interest in the Baptism in the Holy Spirit, so the Protestants may one day express gratitude to the Catholics for bringing to the Movement the highest ecclesiastical approbation it has thus far received in this country, after years of getting bruises. For example, several years ago, when Father Dennis Bennett, of Van Nuys, was setting California Episcopalians on fire with the Spirit, James A. Pike, then Episcopal bishop of California, issued a pastoral letter in which he said this about tongues: "This particular phenomenon has reached a point where it is dangerous to the power and unity of the church and a threat to sound doctrine and policy." He referred to tongues as "heresy in embryo," directing the clergy to discourage it and advising laymen not to seek it. Things like this did not do much to endear the church to Jesus People, and when I asked some Episcopalian Jesus People about it, they said: "Yeah, but look what happened to Pike. He got strung out on a spirit-world trip, trying to make contact with his son who had committed suicide; and then he died out on the Jordanian desert, trying to find the Essene monastery where some people think Jesus spent his hidden years."

Most churches were torn apart by internal strife over the Jesus Movement. Only the Catholic Church seemed to have little to say. It became known, however, that in 1967 the National Conference of Catholic Bishops appointed Bishop Alexander Zaleski, of Lansing, Michigan, to head a committee to investigate the Movement as it was beginning to exhibit itself among the Catholic Pentecostals. The report was submitted in November, 1969, but it was not made public for more than another year. It said, in part:

"It must be admitted that theologically the movement has legitimate reasons for existence. It has a strong biblical basis. It would be difficult to inhibit the work of the Spirit which manifested itself so abundantly in the early Church. The participants in the Catholic Pentecostal movement claim that they receive certain charismatic gifts. Admittedly, there have been abuses, but the cure is not a denial of their existence but their proper use. We still need further research on the matter of the charismatic gifts. Certainly, the recent Vatican Council presumes that the Spirit is active continuously in the Church.

"Perhaps our most prudent way to judge the validity of the claim of the Pentecostal Movement is to observe the effects on those who participate in the prayer meetings. There are many indications that this participation leads to a better understanding of the role the Christian plays in the Church. Many have experienced progress in their spiritual life. They are attracted to the readings of the scriptures and a deeper understanding of their faith. They seem to grow in their attachment to certain established devotional patterns such as devotions to the real presence and the rosary.

"It is the conclusion of the Committee on Doctrine that the movement should at this point not be inhibited but allowed to develop. . . ."

Although the statement pertained to Catholics, and althought it did state that Protestants may be a bit emotional in their meetings, it was, I felt, a statement regarding the entire Jesus People Movement. On my trip, I attended both Protestant and Catholic prayer meetings, with members of each denomination present at the meetings of the other. Maybe the Protestants were emotional, which I liked at Calvary Chapel and didn't like as much at Bethel Tabernacle. Otherwise, people were just being Christians, worshipping together in the Spirit, and it was beautiful.

I buy it.

On the trip, I saw and heard some things that disquieted me, but perhaps this was because these things were new to me and I did not understand them. I heard some testimonies that changed in detail when I went over them a second or third time, but these were few and unimportant. Some of the things a few of the leaders told me about themselves did not agree with some of the printed material I examined when I got to that part of my research, but these areas were few, too, and unimportant. Also, I felt that some of the anti-church sentiments expressed by some of the leaders were more the results of personal wounds than personal convictions. Since my trip, I have read that some leaders have accused Jesus People of copping out by entering the mainstreams of church life. Where are people going to go? They can't all live in communes, although they can all live in community.

There is just one area where I still have mixed feelings, and this is the matter of the End Times. I agreed with Ralph Martin, in Ann Arbor, that the Second Coming is such an important Christian tenet that the concern among Protestants about the End Times cannot be written off. At the same time, however, I remember a remark by Pope John XXIII: "God did not create the world so that men could turn it into a cemetery." I remember, too, the theory of Pierre Tielhard de Chardin who believed that all things in the world came of Jesus the Alpha and that the world would return to Jesus the Omega, and that this was a forward-moving journey, that evolution has actually been a provolution, that man did not descend from apes but ascended from them, and that all these billions of years have been a cleansing period, allowing men, through love and brotherhood and good works, to conquer evil, perfecting the world as we proceed toward Jesus and his Second Coming. I suppose this makes me sound unrealistically optimistic, but you must remember that for twenty years I have been working for the creator of *The Power of Positive Thinking*. Dr. Peale and we have got our rights.

As for the rest of me, I leave that to the Lord.

D

June 28, 77			